Twelve Short Plays and One Long One

Ideal for College Drama Departments, Community Theaters and Even Off Broadway

TWELVE SHORT PLAYS AND ONE LONG ONE

IDEAL FOR COLLEGE DRAMA DEPARTMENTS, COMMUNITY THEATERS AND EVEN OFF BROADWAY

MELVYN CHASE

SUNSTONE PRESS

SANTA FE

FOR PERFORMANCE RIGHTS, CONTACT:
Melvyn Chase (203) 372-2517
melvynchase@optonline.net

Sunstone books may be purchased for educational, business, or sales promotional use.
For information please write: Special Markets Department, Sunstone Press,
P.O. Box 2321, Santa Fe, New Mexico 87504-2321.
Printed on acid-free paper
∞

Library of Congress Cataloging-in-Publication Data

Names: Chase, Melvyn, 1938- author.
Title: Twelve short plays and one long one : ideal for college drama
    departments, community theaters and even off Broadway / Melvyn Chase.
Description: Santa Fe : Sunstone Press, [2023] | Summary: "Twelve one-act
    plays, some serious, some comedic, ideally suited for classes in acting
    and directing"-- Provided by publisher.
Identifiers: LCCN 2023035030 | ISBN 9781632935564 (paperback) | ISBN
    9781611397260 (epub)
Subjects: LCGFT: Drama.
Classification: LCC PS3603.H3794 T94 2023 | DDC 812.6--dc23/eng/20230809
LC record available at https://lccn.loc.gov/2023035030

WWW.SUNSTONEPRESS.COM
SUNSTONE PRESS / POST OFFICE BOX 2321 / SANTA FE, NM 87504-2321 /USA
(505) 988-4418

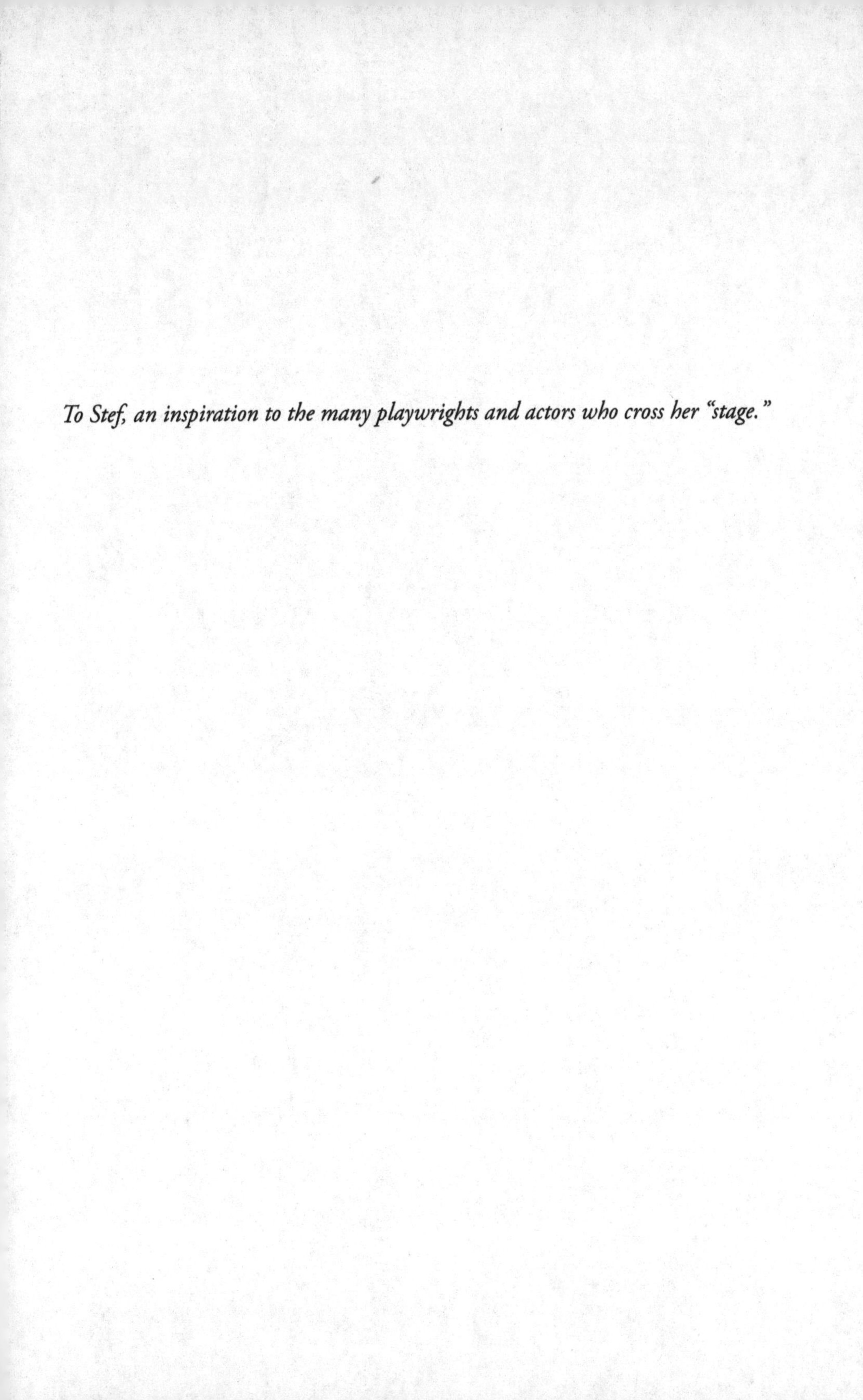

To Stef, an inspiration to the many playwrights and actors who cross her "stage."

Contents

Introduction

This unique collection of twelve one-act plays is ideally suited for classes in acting and directing. Most of the pieces are two-handers, some serious, some comedic. By design, the format is simple and flexible, allowing for effective classroom performances without sets or props, and with a minimum of stage business. Importantly, each play can also serve as the foundation for a variety of creative interpretations—an excellent starting point for classroom discussions and critiques. Beyond the classroom, the collection is also a valuable resource for community theater groups planning an evening of one-act plays.

A word about the origin of these plays. For more than two decades, Stephanie Campion, a British ex-pat living in Paris, has organized live readings of new plays with casts of professional actors. After the readings, the audience is invited to join the actors in an exchange of ideas, critiquing the plays and providing feedback on "what works—and what doesn't."

During the COVID-19 pandemic, when theaters all over the world went dark, Stef switched these readings to an online medium: Zoom. This transition enabled her to include playwrights, actors and audiences worldwide, from Europe and North America—via South Africa—all the way to New Zealand.

Because of the technological constraints of performing on Zoom, the plays were tightly written, usually for only two or three actors, with the drama or comedy primarily driven by the verbal interaction of the characters. The one-act plays in this collection were written by Melvyn Chase for readings on Zoom.

As a special feature, this collection also includes Chase's full-length drama, "Home Bodies," which had a live reading in Paris.

TRUTH WEARING THE COMIC MASK

THE BIRD OF TIME

CHARACTERS:

CHARLIE DREW, *an unpublished author in his late twenties. He is unprepossessing, polite, but* not *timid.*
LUCY DAVIS, *an artist in her late twentiess. She is aggressive, self-confident, argumentative.*

THE TIME: *An afternoon in May.*
THE PLACE: *Washington Square Park, Greenwich Village, N.Y.*

As the action begins, LUCY *is seated on a park bench.* CHARLIE *approaches her.*

CHARLIE. (*politely*) Do you mind if I sit here?

LUCY. (*snidely*) You think I own this bench? Or maybe I rent it? Don't be such an a-hole. You don't need my permission.

CHARLIE. Well, I just figured you might want a little privacy...

(*He sits down on the bench.*)

LUCY. If I wanted (*air quotes*) "a little privacy," would I be sitting on my ass, on a sunny Spring day like this, in the middle of Washington Square Park—surrounded by thousands of people? No, I don't think so. I'd be hunched down in a dark cave somewhere, contemplating my navel. Or sequestered in a nunnery... praying for your benighted soul.

CHARLIE. A "nunnery," huh? I like that. Very Shakespearean. Hamlet's line to Ophelia, right? "Get thee to a nunnery, go." But, as you probably know, what *he* meant by a "nunnery" was... a "brothel." (*pause*) Hmm... I guess *that* could be kind of lonely, too. Psychologically speaking.

LUCY. Hey, I don't mind you sitting here—but that doesn't mean I want to be your Best Friend Forever. And I don't care what Shakespeare meant. Okay? I also don't care what *you* mean. I'm not in the mood for conversation.

CHARLIE. Yeah, you look like you're really angry about something.

LUCY. I am *always* angry about something. And you know why? Because whatever I do, wherever I go, there's always some goddamn thing to be angry about. Like right now!

CHARLIE. Okay, okay. (*raising his hands in surrender*) I promise: I won't say another word.

(*Long pause*)

LUCY. (*reluctantly, her curiosity piqued*) One question, though. I see you've got a suitcase with you, so I guess you're going somewhere—or coming from somewhere?

CHARLIE. No, I'm not traveling anywhere.

LUCY. (*her antennae suddenly up*) Uh-oh! You're not homeless are you? Dragging around everything you own in one lousy suitcase? Because, believe me, I'm not picking up any stray cats! No way!

CHARLIE. I'm not a stray *anything*. I've got a nice pad on Jane Street. Fourth floor, with elevator.

LUCY. So what's with the suitcase?

CHARLIE. I thought you said you weren't in the mood for conversation. Have you noticed *you're* the one doing all the talking?

LUCY. All right, all right. *Mea culpa.* I lied. So what's with the suitcase? It's not a bomb is it? I don't want to die for your "cause"—whatever it is—or anybody else's.

CHARLIE. It's not a bomb. It's my book.

LUCY. Your book? You're carrying around a book in a suitcase? I'm sorry I asked.

CHARLIE. It isn't just "*a*" book. It's the manuscript of a book I *wrote*. My first novel. And the way things are going, it could be my last!

LUCY. And I suppose you can't leave it home because *it* gets... lonely?

CHARLIE. (*ignoring her comment*) It's called (*with pride*) "The Bird of Time."

LUCY. (*teasing*) Let me guess: it's the little cuckoo in a clock, right?

CHARLIE. (*still ignoring her*) In the "Rubaiyat of Omar Khayyam"... there's this quatrain:
> "Come, fill the Cup, and in the Fire of Spring
> "The Winter Garment of Repentance fling:
> "The Bird of Time has but a little way
> "To flutter, and the Bird is on the Wing."

LUCY. (*nodding, approvingly*) Okay, that's nice.

CHARLIE. (*with enthusiasm*) And listen to this: The book is about *one* hour—just one *critical* hour—of *one* day—in the lives of 28 different people. And how that one hour *affects* their lives—and the world around them. (*with rising enthusiasm*) And they're all from different countries—and different times in the past. Second-century Jerusalem. Kansas during World War I. Paris during the French Revolution.

LUCY. And you know enough to write about all that crap?

CHARLIE. (*proudly*) Elementary, my dear Watson. Research. Tons and tons of research. (*sighs*) I've been working on this book for almost four years.

LUCY. Wow! My hat's off to you. You've got grit. But why are you carrying around the manuscript in a suitcase?

CHARLIE. It's the only way I *can* carry it. It's *very* long. One thousand seven hundred and fifty-six typed pages, twelve-point Verdana...*double* spaced.

LUCY. (*pretending to be helpful*) That's a *big* bird! You know, if you *single*-spaced, it might fit into an overnight bag. It would be a lot easier to handle. (*changing tone*) But you still haven't told me *why* you're carrying it around.

CHARLIE. I've sent cover letters and sample chapters to every goddamn publisher in the universe. And every goddamn agent. And nobody's interested in my book. Nobody wants to give it a chance. Or *read* it. Nobody.

LUCY. That's an awful lot of reading. They may not have a month to spare.

CHARLIE. Well, today I decided to try a new approach. I took my manuscript to Edwin Gardner's office on West 4th Street. (He's a big-time agent.) I wanted him to turn me down face-to-face.

LUCY. Did you actually get to see him? Face-to-face?

CHARLIE. Yes. He was very pleasant. And...he turned me down.

LUCY. (*with genuine sympathy*) So what are you going to do now? Drag your book around to every publisher in town, so you can get shot down in person?

CHARLIE. Honestly, I don't know what else I can do.

LUCY. Have you thought about *self*-publishing? Lots of writers are doing that.

CHARLIE. Yes, I've thought about it. I have. But I can't do it. I'd be admitting that I've failed.

(*Long pause*)

LUCY. You said you've been working on your book for four years. Bussing tables? Walking dogs? Free-lancing to pay the rent?

CHARLIE. No, I was writing full time, every day, day after day.

LUCY. So you have enough money to do that, huh? Lucky guy.

CHARLIE. No, I'm not rich. But my *parents* are. They own a funeral "emporium" in Greenwich, Connecticut. It's a thriving business.

LUCY. Yeah. I know... A lot of people are dying to get into it.

CHARLIE. Ha! Anyway, that's my story. There's four years of my life in this suitcase. A great novel. Unique. One-of-a-kind. And going absolutely nowhere.

LUCY. (*after a polite pause, in a friendly way*) By the way, I'm Lucy Davis. What's *your* name?

CHARLIE. Charlie. Charlie Drew. Nice to meet you, Lucy.

LUCY. Same here. And Charlie, as it happens, I understand exactly where you're coming from. In fact, I'm in the same boat: up shit's creek without a paddle.

CHARLIE. You're a writer, too?

LUCY. No. I'm an artist—a painter. A damn good one! But I can't get a gallery to show my paintings. Or an art magazine to do a profile. I can't even get a *semi-influential* critic to look at my work. Or some rich collector to sponsor me. And you know, in my world, it's *those* people who make you or break you. Great art is what *they* say it is.

CHARLIE. I get the picture (if you'll pardon the expression).

LUCY. I'm not lucky enough to have parents in the funeral business. But my sister Olivia writes children's books and I illustrate them. To be honest with you, I hate children! They're all real cute and cuddly when they're little, but when they grow up, most of them turn out to be *people*—greedy and stupid.

CHARLIE. Present company excepted, of course.

LUCY. Olivia and I don't make a fortune but it's enough to keep us in bed and board—in a loft on Macdougal Street.

CHARLIE. But if you're an artist with published work, what's the problem? You must have a reputation.

LUCY. Oh, I've got one all right. The people who count in the art world have decided that I'm *not* a painter—I'm *not* an artist—I'm just an "illustrator." They won't take me seriously.

CHARLIE. Yeah, I guess we *are* in the same leaky boat.

LUCY. Well, to be honest, I *do* have one other problem. It's what you might call my "personality."

CHARLIE. Well, you *are* a little "touchy."

LUCY. Actually, I'm a lot worse than that. I can't help it. I've tried. But it's *who* I am. *What* I am. I had high hopes when I entered the Rhode Island School of Design. Good school, looks great on a resumé. And granted, I learned a lot there. But I quit. Dropped out in my third year 'cause I got tired of them telling me what to do. Like I said, that's *me*! I *knew* what I wanted to do. I just wanted them to show me *how* to do it. They didn't. I got mad, yelled a lot, made a lot of enemies. So I picked up my brushes and walked away. And the same thing happened, over and over again, when I tried to make contacts with other artists—with agents—with critics—with gallery owners. I just can't play the game. I can't kiss ass. And I'm paying for it.

CHARLIE. Well, at least you aren't carrying your paintings around in a suitcase!

LUCY. Hah! So my cloud has a silver lining! (*getting serious*) Hey...wait a minute...maybe *yours* does, too. I think there could be a way I can help you.

CHARLIE. You want to illustrate my book?

LUCY. No, but Olivia and I have an agent. A good one. Dennis Connors. He likes her and he *seems* to like me.

CHARLIE. You mean, someone who can help you actually *likes* you?

LUCY. Well, once in a while... Anyway, I'm pretty sure we can get him to read your book. Not the whole goddamn thing, of course. Just the first five hundred pages, or so. And maybe—if he likes it—maybe—look, I can't promise you anything—but *maybe* he'll represent you.

CHARLIE. That would be great! And you know, I just might be able to return the favor.

LUCY. Let me guess: your parents just did a star-studded red-carpet funeral for a celebrity art critic, and his only surviving son—a gallery owner himself (what are the odds!)—swore eternal gratitude.

CHARLIE. Better than that. I have an aunt—Aunt Margaret—Maggie— my mother's sister. She's the black sheep of the family.

LUCY. Why? They offered her a partnership in the funeral home, but she said she didn't dig it?

CHARLIE. Lucy! *Listen* to me. My Aunt Margaret is a lot like you. All her life, she's managed to piss everybody off. Her parents. Her three ex-husbands. Her two ex-wives. Even my mother, who insists on loving her anyway. But Maggie's always had a soft spot in her heart for me—because I'm a struggling artist. And she *loves* struggling artists. Up until a year ago, she managed a gallery in San Francisco where she gave young painters—

unknowns—a chance to show their work. She just moved back to New York and opened a little "boutiquey" gallery of her own in Soho. So if you don't piss each other off too much—and if she likes your paintings—I can't make any promises—but...

LUCY. That would be wonderful.

CHARLIE. You know...this is just like my book. The two of us meet by chance. Total strangers. And suddenly, in an hour, our lives go in new directions. An agent for me—I hope. A gallery for you—I hope.

LUCY. Yeah, you're right. The formula really seems to be working for us. You know, I'm thinking maybe I should get to know more about your book—first-hand—*before* I talk to Dennis.

CHARLIE. (*unenthusiastically*) You do? Well...maybe...

LUCY. I mean, he's sure to ask me if I've read it, isn't he?

CHARLIE. (*still very hesitant*) I guess...yeah, he might...

LUCY. Hey: believe me, I don't intend to read the whole damn thing! Just enough so I don't sound stupid when he asks me about it. What's the problem?

CHARLIE. I don't know... It's just that...

LUCY. You've been working on this freaking book for four years, right? You want people to read it, don't you?

CHARLIE. Yes, of course I do.

LUCY. Well, *I'm* people, aren't I?

CHARLIE. Yes, but... I mean, you're *very* judgmental.

LUCY. Judgmental? *Moi*? Where in the world did you ever get *that* idea?

NICKY TELLS ALL

CHARACTERS:
JENNIFER LOGAN, *a young, eager reporter for PEOPLE magazine.*
"NICKY DAMON," *an "infamous celebrity."*

THE TIME: *Recently.*
THE PLACE: *A luxury apartment.*

The doorbell rings.

NICKY. Come in, Ms. Logan. Sit down, get cozy.

JENNIFER. (*very nervously*) Cozy? Uh—Thank you, Mr. Damon.

NICKY. Please call me Nicky.

JENNIFER. Okay. I'm Jenny.

NICKY. Would you like a glass of wine, Jenny?

JENNIFER. I really shouldn't, Mr....uh...Nicky. I get a little sleepy...

NICKY. I must say—and I don't mean to offend you—but you're not at all what I expected.

JENNIFER. (*still very tentative*) Well, neither are *you.*

NICKY. That's kind of my stock in trade. Despite all the stories about me—

nonsense, most of them—I really hate to be obvious. But—I expected to be interviewed by someone more—*mature*. I mean, this is really a big story for PEOPLE Magazine, isn't it?

JENNIFER. (*sighs*) It is—and it isn't.

NICKY. (*sternly*) Meaning what?

JENNIFER. Well, you see... Nobody at the office took it seriously.

NICKY. I can't believe it! This is the only interview I have *ever* given! *My* side of the story, for the first time! And it's a hell of a story. It's "stop-the-presses" news! And nobody gives a damn?

JENNIFER. I'm sorry, Nicky. But you know there are fewer and fewer True Believers out there.

NICKY. That's for sure. So tell me: how long have you been working for PEOPLE?

JENNIFER. About six months.

NICKY. And who have you interviewed so far?

JENNIFER. Well, I mostly do background stuff.

NICK. For example?

JENNIFER. I had a great session with Justin Bieber's driver. Very informative.

NICKY. Life in the rear-view mirror... How illuminating.

JENNIFER. And Tom Hanks's kindergarten teacher.

NICKY. And now...me.

JENNIFER. My boss said this would be my baptism by fire.

NICKY. That's a well-chosen metaphor.

JENNIFER. She kind of laughed when she said it. Everyone did.

NICKY. (*with an evil look in his eyes*) Who knows? Perhaps someday *I'll* have the *last* laugh. And what about you, Jenny? Do you think I'm a joke?

JENNIFER. Oh... I think I'll reserve judgment on that.

NICKY. And if you believe me?

JENNIFER. (*with a show of confidence in herself*) It'll be a great story. I'll tell the world!

NICKY. Good girl.

JENNIFER. But that doesn't mean the *world* will believe me.

NICKY. Well, we can make a damn good try, can't we? Let's begin.

JENNIFER. Okay. Uh—Would you mind if I record this? It's easier than taking notes.

NICKY. Not at all. Not in the least.

JENNIFER. Well, then... Go back, Nicky. As far back as you can remember. Your earliest memories...

NICKY. Uh-huh...(*slowly, thoughtfully*) In the beginning... (to borrow a phrase)... Before there were planets or stars... Before there was space or time... Before there was *anything*... there was Light... Light everywhere... Warm and pure... Washing over you, an endless waterfall of Light.

JENNIFER. If this is before there was anything...where *were* you?

NICKY. We were with The Boss. And I don't mean *Bruce Springsteen*. I mean *The* Boss. In *His* space.

JENNIFER. You said "we"?

NICKY. There were lots of us—an army of us. I don't know how many. But I *do* know this: I was special. I was The Boss's right hand man. The second in command. Well, maybe I'm exaggerating a little.

JENNIFER. You mean you didn't actually command anyone?

NICKY. God forbid!

JENNIFER. So what was so special about you?

NICKY. (*proudly*) He made me the Light-bearer. In the beginning, that was my name. Before there was a universe, there was nothing else *but* the Light, and The Boss gave *me* the Light—and when he created the suns— the stars—the galaxies—I brought them their Light! I set them ablaze! And they're still burning!

JENNIFER. So it was *you* we should thank for sunlight and moonlight and starlight.

NICKY. Yes, the buck stops here.

JENNIFER. But that's not the whole story, is it? What went wrong.

NICKY. A lot of things.

(*He hesitates, frowns, but doesn't answer.*)

JENNIFER. What kind of things?

NICKY. I have to admit that I got a little light-headed. (Pardon the play on words.) Or maybe I should say *swell*-headed.

JENNIFER. I don't blame you. Sounds like you had a really important job.

NICKY. And a lot of admirers. I enjoyed the fact that they looked up to me.

JENNIFER. Isn't that a sin?

NICKY. Pride? I think it's one of the biggies.

JENNIFER. So that was your *first* problem.

NICKY. That, plus the fact that I started to attract—I don't know what I'd call it. I guess you could say it was a fan club.

JENNIFER. The Boss didn't like that.

NICKY. He hated it. But that wasn't my biggest problem.

JENNIFER. What *was*?

NICKY. Nepotism, Jenny. Plain, old-fashioned nepotism.

JENNIFER. You'll have to explain that.

NICKY. Way back when, in the Renaissance, some Popes were not quite as devout as they should have been. Lo and behold, they had children! They said their bastard sons were their nephews—"*nepos*" in Latin. And they made sure those "nephews" got the best jobs—made the most money.

JENNIFER. You had trouble with nephews?

NICKY. Worse. With a Son. The Boss's Son.

JENNIFER. I'm beginning to understand.

NICKY. Picture this: I'm the Light-bearer. I set the stars on fire. I'm the Boss's right-hand man. Then, suddenly, I'm *not*. Because suddenly, the universe has become a *family* business. I was almost at the top of the Org Chart, and then I was kicked downstairs. It was hard to take.

JENNIFER. Did you tell The Boss how you felt?

NICKY. I didn't have to. He's omniscient.

JENNIFER. He wasn't pleased?

NICKY. That's putting it mildly. You know the Good-Cop/Bad-Cop routine? Well, His Son—as everyone knows—is very forgiving, but *He* is not. And it wasn't just *me* He was mad at: it was my fan club. My "people" were grumbling, complaining.

JENNIFER. Did you try to warn them?

NICKY. Mmm... Guess I should have. But I was angry. Frustrated. I just fed the flames. I was their leader. We rebelled against The Boss. And of course, we lost.

JENNIFER. That must have been awful.

NICKY. It was—and it wasn't.

JENNIFER. What do you mean?

NICKY. We had lost *His* kingdom, but we had a chance to start a new kingdom from scratch. A place we could call our own. A place where *we'd* make the rules.

JENNIFER. "Better to reign in Hell than serve in Heaven"?

NICKY. Well, maybe not *better*. But you've got to make the most of your opportunities. And we did. We built our new world from the ground down. And we came to love it.

JENNIFER. How can anyone love Hell?

NICKY. Granted, it took a while. But forever is a long, long time.

JENNIFER. Let me ask you this: Why do you hate us so much? Why are you our Enemy?

NICKY. I hate you because *He* loves you. It's as simple as that.

JENNIFER. So you became a snake and tempted Eve and really screwed things up for us.

NICKY. First of all, that never happened. It's just a story—a way to explain why people aren't perfect—why the world isn't perfect. Like it's *your* fault. So it helps to keep you in line.

JENNIFER. No Adam and Eve. No surprise there.

NICKY. If that story *were* true, I sure as hell wouldn't appear as a snake. I don't like snakes. Who does? I would have been a kind of cross between a lizard and a man... Like the GEICO Gekko, but more dignified.

JENNIFER. But it didn't happen.

NICKY. Of course not. The Boss put all the right ingredients together on a brand new planet—the one you call home. He lit the spark of life, and let Evolution take over. And you know, there were a lot of *almost-humans* in the game before you, and even *after* you showed up. Like the Neanderthals.

JENNIFER. (*playing along*) But we outlasted them all.

NICKY. Well, you were smarter, better organized and—let's face it— meaner, too. Now and then your boys had a toss in the hay with one of the *almost*-women. (There's no accounting for taste.) And you still have some Neanderthal in you. And a trace of the other almost-humans. But *they're* all long gone.

JENNIFER. So that's the *real* story.

NICKY. It is. But you know, even Genesis got it wrong.

JENNIFER. What do you mean?

NICKY. The Fall of Man isn't what it's cracked up to be. It isn't really a tragedy.

JENNIFER. You've *got* to be kidding.

NICKY. I'm not. Just imagine the Garden of Eden. Is it some kind of paradise? Sure, the weather was great. Plenty to eat. There were no worries. No work. Lots of free time. But think about this: if Adam and Eve didn't know the difference between good and evil—if they were always obedient, always following the rules in lockstep, never raising a "point of order," were they any better than the other creatures in the Garden? Or were they just glorified animals, at the top of the food chain?

JENNIFER. I suppose that's one way to look at it.

NICKY. The fact is: *knowing* what is good and *doing* good are two very different things. You don't need devils to tempt you, or contracts signed in blood. "The Devil made me do it?" *Puh-leeze.* You do a pretty messy job of it yourself, without any help from us.

JENNIFER. I guess you could say that.

NICKY. Your animal side is always at war with your human side. And the animal side racks up a lot of wins.

JENNIFER. (*defensively*) Okay, okay. But getting back to *you*, what about the afterlife? Fire. Brimstone. Torture. You love that stuff, don't you?

NICKY. Another myth. There are no demons with pitchforks. No flames. That's just a way to scare people into being good—whether they like it or not.

JENNIFER. Then what *is* Hell?

NICKY. It's knowing that you'll never, *ever* taste the pleasures of Paradise. And that's damnation enough for anyone.

JENNIFER. And what *are* the pleasures of Paradise?

NICKY. (*sadly*) I have no idea. I've never been there. Never *will* be there. But that's not what eats at me. For me, Hell is knowing I was so close to The Boss—that I was the Light-bearer—and I'll never be that again.

(*He stops... and then, suddenly, with devilish eyes smoldering, voice deepening, chest heaving, he waits for JENNIFER to ask another question.*)

NICKY. So... Anything else?

JENNIFER. (*mesmerized, trance-like*) I don't...really...have any...more questions.

NICKY. (*calmer, less menacing*) Do you believe me, Jenny?

JENNIFER. (*shaken*) I don't...know. But I want to write your story.

NICKY. (*smiles*) That's good enough for me.

JENNIFER. Thank you, Nicky.

NICKY. Thank *you*, Jenny. Goodbye and may I wish you "Godspeed."

(*After a pause, JENNIFER, in a professional tone, speaks to the audience.*)

JENNIFER. I wasn't sure how I felt when I left Nicky. Confused, of course. I mean, how could all this be true? But I thought I had a hell of a story—if it got published. It was late at night when I went to the office to transcribe the interview. I turned on the tape recorder and—*nothing*. I played the whole thing, both sides. Nothing. The tape was blank, from start to finish. I know I had switched the recorder on. The little red light was definitely lit. I remembered a lot of what Nicky said, but there were some great direct quotes I really needed. I should have taken notes. An experienced reporter would have done that. Could I try to see Nicky again and write everything down next time? Would he see me again? I called his number. A recorded voice told me "This number is not in service." I didn't hesitate. I went back to the apartment building. When I rang the doorbell, an elderly woman answered. I could see past her to the interior of the apartment. It was the kind of place an elderly woman would love—in no way Nicky's style. And then suddenly it was all so clear. I decided to tell my boss what she wanted to hear: the story wasn't worth publishing. Nicky was just a strange man with "serious delusions." That would please my boss. But, more important, it would please *The* Boss.

POLES APART

CHARACTERS:
DAVID TENNYSON FORSYTHE, *a pompous BBC TV reporter.*
MAXIMILIAN, *an elf in Santa's Workshop, who tells it like it is.*

THE TIME: *Christmas Day.*
THE PLACE: *Santa's Workshop at the North Pole.*

FORSYTHE. *(introducing his TV show)* Good evening. I'm David Tennyson Forsythe of the BBC. Here we are. It's Christmas Day and, for all of us—young and old—tall and tiny—rich and relatively poor—it's a jolly, jolly time. A time for sharing this joyous season with those we love— and even with those we dislike. We're busy exchanging inappropriate and unappreciated gifts. Imbibing inordinate quantities of Christmas cheer. And perhaps feasting on a savory, Dickensian Christmas-Carol goose. God bless us every one!

But alas—if truth be told—for some few, it is a season tinged with a recurring holiday anxiety. Especially for those reporters, like myself, who must *somehow* find a "new angle" for this year's "Christmas story." Oh, of course, I have had my triumphs in the past. Three years ago, my tale of gifts returned unopened—many complete with bow and wrapping paper still undisturbed—won kudos for originality. And last year, I broke new ground for *chutzpah* with my acclaimed feature on the Yule-tide activities of convicts on Death Row.

But this year, as the holiday season approached, it seemed as if the well had run dry. What, after all, hadn't already been said of Father Christmas—

Santa Claus—Saint Nicholas—whatever you wish to call him? His wife—his reindeer—his "naughty or nice" lists—his amazing antics on rooftops and up-and-down chimneys—all of this has been covered from top to bottom—in prose—in poetry—in song and story—in films and on the telly. What's a reporter to do? (*smiling, brightening*) And then, like Archimedes in his bathtub, I had my "Eureka moment." Why not get up close and personal with one of the unsung heroes of Father Christmas's workshop? One of the diminutive toy-builders—the elves who make children's dreams come true. (*proudly*) And so, accompanied by my camera crew, I flew to the North Pole and, during a lunch break at the factory, I interviewed an elf. And what a revelation it was! Maximilian was not your ordinary elf. Let's roll the tape...

MAXIMILIAN. (*looking around suspiciously*) Does *he* know you're doing this?

FORSYTHE. You mean Father Christmas?

MAXIMILIAN. Yeah, yeah. The fat "ho-ho-ho" guy.

FORSYTHE. Well, he gave me *carte blanche*. I don't even have to clear the final version with him.

MAXIMILIAN. (*under his breath*) That's just like him. So sure of himself.

FORSYTHE. What did you say?

MAXIMILIAN. Nothing, nothing. Let's get going. I only have forty minutes. Not a second more.

FORSYTHE. (*surprised*) It sounds like they're rather strict here.

MAXIMILIAN. Tell me about it.

FORSYTHE. Then I guess I'd better forge ahead. To begin with, Maximilian, I'm surprised that all of you are so—*large*.

MAXIMILIAN. Hah! You thought we're a bunch of happy little elves?

That's just a marketing gimmick—and it works. It makes for a nice story. But believe me, in this job, you've got to be big and strong to survive.

FORSYTHE. Is the work you do really that hard?

MAXIMILIAN. (*laughs nastily*) Yeah, it is, but it *shouldn't* be.

FORSYTHE. What do you mean?

MAXIMILIAN. It's ridiculous: we're still making toys the old-fashioned way. With hammers and saws and sandpaper—the way we did a hundred—two hundred—*three* hundred years ago. The rest of the world is into mass production—assembly lines—computers—robots. But not *our* shop. So tell me, why haven't we done that? It would make our lives a hell of a lot easier.

FORSYTHE. Well, why *haven't* you modernized your factory?

MAXIMILIAN. (*bitterly*) Because the fat old man in the red suit is in love with *Tradition*.

FORSYTHE. That seems a bit unfair.

MAXIMILIAN. A *bit*? Do you know how many freaking toys we make in a year?

FORSYTHE. I can't imagine...

MAXIMILIAN. Well, neither can I. But we're at it eight hours every day, January to December, every year. You know, Rudolph works one night a year. *One night*. And he's got a hit song, and television shows and action figures. He's a freaking industry! You could easily replace his "shiny red nose" with a GPS. But you can't replace *us*.

FORSYTHE. An excellent argument.

MAXIMILIAN. And there are lots of other characters that hog the Christmas spotlight: The Grinch! Frosty the Freaking Snowman. Good

Old Charlie Brown! And here we are, every day, working our freezing tails off, and *they* get all the publicity—and all the loving!

FORSYTHE. How sad. You say you work all year. There's no vacation time?

MAXIMILIAN. Oh, yeah. We get two weeks in August.

FORSYTHE. So you have a chance to relax, perhaps to travel.

MAXIMILIAN. Uh-huh. We usually go to Greenland, to soak up the sun.

FORSYTHE. Why not someplace a little warmer? The Riviera, perhaps? The Costa del Sol? Or Florida?

MAXIMILIAN. Hah! Sounds nice, but who can afford it?

FORSYTHE. You're suggesting that you're not well paid.

MAXIMILIAN. Well paid? The last time we got a raise was two days after the Battle of Waterloo! It's been a while.

FORSYTHE. I should say so. Speaking of the past, Max, does your elf-hood go back generations? Did your parents work in the factory, too? Your grandparents?

MAXIMILIAN. Oh, yeah. All of us go way back. I guess you could say, for as long as anyone can remember, "Toys R Us." (That's an old elf joke.)

FORSYTHE. (*pretending to laugh*) Ha! How amusing. And I wonder—are your children carrying on the tradition?

MAXIMILIAN. Nah. We can't hold onto them any more. The kids get on the Internet and see the way the rest of the world lives. Most of them have gone with the wind. I mean, do you blame them? If you had a choice, would you hang around here, freezing your tail off in a dead-end job?

FORSYTHE. On a more personal level, have *your* children left?

MAXIMILIAN. You bet they have. My daughter Laura, the oldest, was the first to go. You know, up here, the kids start skiing right after they start walking. So it was easy for Laura to land a job as a ski instructor in Lake Tahoe. She calls once in a while. She's having a ball. She says she loves *toying* with men's affections. She thinks that's funny. And my son Daniel—well, we worry about him.

FORSYTHE. Why so?

MAXIMILIAN. You ever hear of the "Barbie Killer?"

FORSYTHE. (*gasping*) No, I haven't. You mean Daniel's a...?

MAXIMILIAN. *This* is what I mean: Danny worked in the factory for a couple of years. He had some really sharp ideas about a terrific new kind of Fussball. But did he get a chance to do something with it? No. Instead, he got stuck on the Doll Squad.

FORSYTHE. The Doll Squad?

MAXIMILIAN. Hour after hour, day after day, he had to make (*sarcastically*) sweet little dolls, with sweet little faces and sweet little dresses. He was going bonkers. He couldn't eat. He couldn't sleep. He kept having nightmares about turning into a sweet little doll. Finally, he upped and left.

FORSYTHE. But you said something about a "Killer"?

MAXIMILIAN. (*seriously*) There have been stories about random attacks by a mysterious "doll-destroyer." Late at night, someone breaks into toy stores in Reykjavik. And in the morning, all of the dolls—and *only* the dolls—are smashed to smithereens. And the Barbie Dolls—it's so awful, the newspapers here won't even describe what's been done to *them*. A week or two later, the same thing happens in Helsinki. London may be next. Interpol says it's definitely the same M.O. It's the same guy. They call him the "Barbie Killer."

FORSYTHE. And they can't catch him?

MAXIMILIAN. He's unpredictable. He could strike anywhere. At random. He's always one step ahead of them.

FORSYTHE. And you believe your son could be the Barbie Killer.

MAXIMILIAN. Danny's a travel agent. He could easily hit spots anywhere in the world. We don't know if he's the Barbie Killer, but if he isn't, he's the Killer's biggest fan.

FORSYTHE. A remarkable story, Max. But let's get back to *your* story. You are clearly a very unhappy elf and, by my lights, you have good reason to be. Have you voiced your complaints to Father Christmas?

MAXIMILIAN. We have, but he hasn't paid much attention to us, so I'm changing the rules of engagement.

FORSYTHE. I take it you've devised a new approach to the problem?

MAXIMILIAN. I sure have. You know, we're very competitive. That's part of our elf DNA. You could even call it the *essence* of elf-hood. Every one of us wants to make a better toy than the next guy. Each of us has a unique style all his own. And that's good. But politically, that hurts us. Because we've always complained to the boss *individually*, it's easy for him to brush us off one at a time. So what did I do? I got everybody together for a big meeting and I laid it out for them: "If we don't *organize*, we don't win! Together we've got *E-Power*! *Elf-Power*! Are you with me?"

FORSYTHE. *Were* they with you?

MAXIMILIAN. They sure were—all the way! Tomorrow I'm delivering our petition to the boss—signed by *every* elf—with our list of *demands*. Not "suggestions." Not "proposals." Not "wishes." Demands!

FORSYTHE. What are you "demanding"?

MAXIMILIAN. Demand Number One: Modernize the factory. After all these centuries of back-breaking work, we need better tools to make better toys—and make them more efficiently—and then we can have more free time. Demand Number Two: We want to be paid a living wage. And we want it *now*! Demand Number Three: Give us the credit we deserve for making the dreams of kids come true. (*pause*) Christmas is the season of love and hope: haven't we earned a share of that?

FORSYTHE. I'd say you *have*. But how do you think Father Christmas will respond to your petition?

MAXIMILIAN. (*thoughtfully, without bitterness*) You know, honestly, the old guy really has a heart of gold. But he's so wrapped up in what he's doing—so worried about reaching every child everywhere—that he's forgotten how important *we*—his elves—are. And that's what our petition is really about. Let the world "ooh" and "aah" about Rudolph and the Grinch and Frosty the Freaking Snowman—but remember to put in a good word for the elves that help make it happen. (*pause*) Well, Lunch break is just about over. I've got to get back to work. Nice talking to you. E-Power to the People!

FORSYTHE. E-Power indeed! Thank you, Maximilian, for sharing your thoughts with us. And good luck with your petition. (*to the viewing audience*) To my audience I say, whenever you feel the Christmas Spirit, please put a little love aside for those hard-working elves up at the North Pole, making the toys that brighten the lives of children everywhere. This is David Tennyson Forsythe of the BBC. God bless us—and *them*—every one!

THE SPY

CHARACTER:
HARVEY MOSS, *almost eighty years old, tired of being long past his prime.*

THE TIME: *The present.*
THE PLACE: *The Senior Center.*

HARVEY *addresses the audience directly, as if he were speaking to his friends at the Senior Center.*

HARVEY. You remember two, maybe three weeks ago at the Senior Center? That lecture we heard about growing old "gracefully and gratefully"? Sounds nice, huh? So who gives the lecture? Some perky thirty-year-old woman in a skirt that's a little too short. (Hey, I can dream, can't I?) She doesn't know beans about growing old. How can she?

Oh, yeah, she swore she interviewed *hundreds* of seniors. Good for her! You and I know that old people may complain about a lot of things. But not always the things that *really* bother them. Sure, I hate having all these aches and pains. I pull a muscle and it takes forever to stop hurting. But I can live with that.

Do I miss playing tennis? Not really. I wasn't much of a jock anyway, and after I hurt my shoulder—I was sixty-two or -three—that was all she wrote, brother. I could have had an operation to fix it. But operations are for saving your *life*, not your backhand. Then they went after my prostate. Well... you get the picture.

I'll tell you what the *real* problem is: if you live long enough, the failures of old age make it harder to remember the good things you did when you were young. I'll give you an example...

We were at our daughter Marcia's house for Sunday dinner. When the family gets together, my Edith and I are like footnotes in a book: you can see them at the bottom of the page but you can ignore them. That's us at the dinner table. Everybody is nice enough, but they look past us. Do you blame them? What are we going to talk about? We don't go to work, we don't go to school. We don't read the same books or watch the same movies that our kids and grandkids do. Music? Forget about it! Nat King Cole could be *Old* King Cole as far as they're concerned. Do they give a shit about my latest colonoscopy? But then last Sunday, I had a chance to show off.

The usual suspects were there. Marcia, of course, and her husband David. They own an agency that books accounting and sales temps. (Nowadays, it's beginning to look like *every* job is temporary.) Their daughter Amelia is at Brown University on a *scholarship*! Their thirteen-year-old son Andrew—he's noisy, a little obnoxious—thinks he's King of the World—he was eating everything that wasn't nailed down. *Our* son Michael, the pharmacist—he was there, too, with his girlfriend. I forget her name, but it doesn't matter. They come and go. His bed is like a revolving door.

So all of a sudden, Andrew, the King, makes an announcement.

"Mrs. Ryan, my Social Studies teacher, said that next Thursday is Grandpa's Day."

"Meaning what?" Marcia said.

"We've gotta find out if one of our grandfathers" (he looked at me and said) "well I only have one left—we've gotta find out if our grandfather did anything *amazing* in his life. Something that the class wants to hear about."

"All the grandfathers in one day?"

"No. We're gonna vote on which *three* we want. And after they talk, we'll pick the best one."

He looked at me and, for a change, so did everyone else.

I waited a second—you know, to build up a little suspense—and then I said, "When I was in the army, I was a spy."

Marcia said, "Yes, yes," as if she remembered me telling her about it, a long time ago.

"Here we go again," Edith said. "You know how long it took him to finally tell me what he did in the army? Ten years! Like he was Mata Hari or something."

Andrew frowned and said, "You? A spy?"

"Yes," I whispered.

I knew the kid couldn't believe it. He thought an old fart like me must have been a *young* fart, too.

He said, "Okay. I'll tell them my Grandpa was a spy."

I asked, "Do you want to hear about it?"

"Nah, not now," he said. "Mom, what's for dessert?"

Would you believe it... It turned out I was one of the chosen Grandpas. Andrew told me to be at the school office at 9:45 on Thursday morning.

Edith made me get a haircut and a beard trim. That morning, she gave me a turtleneck sweater, a nice pair of khaki pants—almost new—and she made sure I was wearing matching socks. She even made me shine my shoes.

She said, "Don't slouch. And don't jingle the keys in your pocket."

No man is a hero to his valet. Or his wife. *Especially* his wife.

When the Grandpa trio signed in at the office, we were friendly—but not *too* friendly. After all, we were competing with each other. One of my "opponents" was maybe fifty years old. He had shaved his head but he had a thick red beard. No gray at his age? Probably dyes it. He was super-confident. The other guy was tall and skinny, very tan. He was in his sixties. He had this faraway look in his eye, like he was watching life on another planet.

Mrs. Ryan sent a girl to lead us to the class. Redbeard followed her aggressively. He was already trying to beat us. Tall-and-Thin didn't seem to give a damn. He trailed behind me.

I remembered what it was like in middle school—what we used to call junior high. It was awful. The girls were practically women and the boys were still kids, and everyone was oversexed and in a lousy mood.

Mrs. Ryan was a nice young lady with a pleasant smile. She shook hands with each of us and said, "Welcome, Grandpas. We're looking forward to hearing from you." Then she turned to the kids and said, "Aren't we?"

And they all yelled, "Yessss!!!"

We sat down on chairs that were at the front of the room. Redbeard leaned forward like he was about to launch himself to the moon. Tall-and-Thin leaned back and stared out the window. I tried not to slouch. Mrs. Ryan reminded the kids that in two weeks it was *Grandma's* Day, so they should talk to their grandmothers about *their* lives. Then she called on Alice to introduce her Grandpa. (She was the girl who brought us to the classroom.)

Alice said, "My Grandpa is Tony Foster. He invents video games."

Redbeard jumped out of his chair, hugged Alice, kissed her on the top of the head and pushed her toward her desk. Then he started pacing back and forth, rubbing his *dyed* red beard and looking over his shoulder at the kids.

Suddenly he stopped, faced the class and said, "*Warlock Warriors*. Have you played it?"

Some kids said "Yeah." Some raised their hands.

"*The Valley of Death?*"

More "Yeahs." More raised hands.

He leaned toward them, looking from one face to another.

"*Born to Kill? The Daughters of Darkness? Home from Hell?*"

(I don't really remember what the games were called, but that's what they sounded like to me.)

The kids were practically jumping up and down. "Yeah, yeah, yeah."

Redbeard was all smiles.

He said, "Those are *some* of my babies! And there's plenty more coming!"

A few of the boys cheered.

"Thank you," he said, like he'd just won an Oscar.

He told them that when he was young, he imagined all kinds of places he'd never been—magical worlds where he could be a hero. "And that's what my games do for you," he said. "They make you a hero in magical new worlds." He went on and on, bragging and walking back and forth, rubbing his beard. The kids were eating it up, especially the boys. And he finished with a commercial, plugging his new game, Some kind of fancy-shmantsy spaceship, I think.

A couple of the boys actually applauded. I began to feel a little queasy. But I thought, *These are just games. I can do better than that.*

Mrs. Ryan called on Thomas, who introduced his Grandpa, an archaeologist.

Tall-and-Thin got up very slowly and stood there for a minute or two, not saying anything. Then, all of a sudden, he came to life. He said that he had also dreamed of other worlds when he was a kid. Not make-believe worlds. *Real* ones. Lost worlds. Lost in *time*. And he spent his life looking for them. And finding them!

It turned out he was a hell of a story-teller. He took the kids on a raft with him into the Amazon jungle. Jaguars. Spiders. Snakes. Heat. Danger. And he had actually *found* a lost city. Lost for hundreds of years. He said it was a legend that turned out to be true. The kids were hanging on every word. Mrs. Ryan, too.

Now I was really nervous. I had to make some changes fast. I had to be more exciting. *Scarier*, too. Andrew was at a desk in the front row. He *looked* the way I *felt*.

When he introduced me, he didn't sound like he meant it.

"My Grandpa, Harvey Moss, was a spy."

I tried to relax, but my mouth was dry as a bone.

I said, "When I graduated from college, it was a *dangerous* time." That got their attention.

"The U.S. and Russia were in the middle of what was called the Cold War. Not fighting each other but enemies, just the same. We both had lots of atom bombs. And a war could start anytime. You probably learned about that."

Mrs. Ryan said they *did*.

"There was no freedom in Russia, like there is here. Their government controlled everything. Schools. Farms. Factories. Everything."

They were all listening closely to me. Even Andrew. *Video games. Lost cities. Hah!*

"When I graduated, I joined the army. And I took a very tough test to get into the Army Language School where I studied Russian for a year."

"A whole year?" someone asked. "It's a very hard language to learn," Mrs. Ryan said.

God bless Mrs. Ryan!

"Then you went undercover?" a girl asked. "Parachuted in?" a boy asked. "Made believe you were Russian and learned all kinds of secrets?" "Did you kill anyone?" "How did you get out?"

I wished for Andrew's sake that I *had* parachuted into Moscow and killed a few people. But that wasn't what I did. And I had to tell them that wasn't my job. I explained that I listened to radio messages the Russians were sending to each other. "You can learn a lot that way," I said. "A lot of *important* stuff." But I wasn't the kind of spy they saw in the movies or on TV. I was just listening to radio broadcasts. No guns. No girls. No *sale*.

Andrew wouldn't look at me. Redbeard was stroking his whiskers. Tall-and-Thin was back in the Amazon jungle.

I spent the next few minutes explaining why I was *really*, *actually* a spy. Nobody cared.

That night, I called Andrew. He told me that the voting was very close.

"Who won?"

"The video guy."

"How did *I* do?"

"You got *one* vote."

I said, "Thank you, Andrew."

He said, "It wasn't me. It was Mrs. Ryan."

God Bless Mrs. Ryan!

LEARNING TO LOVE

WHATEVER LOLA WANTS...

CHARACTERS:
JOE MURPHY, *a comedian in his thirties.*
JESSIE MURPHY, *his wife.*

THE TIME: *Three o'clock in the morning.*
THE PLACE: *A hotel room in Las Vegas, Nevada.*

JOE *enters.*

JOE. You didn't have to wait up for me, Jessie. You said you didn't feel well.

JESSIE. I feel better now, Joe. I took a nap. I think I just needed some rest.

JOE. So you're okay?

JESSIE. Uh-huh. How did it go tonight?

JOE. Well, you know: the early show is always a little *iffy*. The high rollers are never there. You get the tourists, the "Gee! Las-Vegas-is-*so*-exciting" crowd. They may have just lost a bundle at the tables, so they're not really in the mood for jokes.

JESSIE. Yeah, that's always a tough sell.

JOE. But you know, Honey, by the end of the act, we were grabbing them. Lola was, anyway. They didn't pay much attention to *me*.

JESSIE. And that always works best for you, doesn't it? When she grabs the spotlight?

JOE. You bet it does. As usual, the second show was better. And the late show turned out to be a real blast!

JESSIE. That good, huh?

JOE. (*enthusiastically*) Here's what happened. Jerry Seinfeld had a table right by the stage and before you know it, he's part of the act!

JESSIE. No kidding?

JOE. We did some bits and the audience was warming up, but you could tell they were waiting for Seinfeld to say something. So we took a chance. Lola calls out to him: "Jerry, what do you think of our act?"

JESSIE. Was he okay with that?

JOE. Oh, yeah. He comes back with, "You know, your act is like my show. It's about 'nothing'." And Lola says, "Only difference is: *your* nothing is worth millions. And ours is worth...*nothing*!"

JESSIE. Did he like that?

JOE. Damn right! He loved it! He roared. And the audience ate it up. He even came backstage after the show. Just to say how much he enjoyed us—especially Lola.

JESSIE. (*without enthusiasm*) Sounds like a good night. A great night, even.

JOE. I'm sorry you missed it, Honey. Listen, I'm exhausted. I'm riding high on fumes right now, but I've got to get some sleep.

JESSIE. Not yet, Joe.

JOE. (*misinterpreting her meaning*) Honestly, Jess, I'm too tired for... smoochin'.

JESSIE. I don't want to make love, Joe. I just want to talk.

JOE. That sounds a little ominous.

JESSIE. No, not "ominous." But "serious."

JOE. Do we have to do this now? Like I said, I'm really tired.

JESSIE. (*meaningfully*) So am I.

JOE. *Ohhh*-kay. What's the problem?

JESSIE. (*deliberately, taking her time*) I was thinking today about when we met.

JOE. (*reluctantly reminiscing*) The Talent Show at the church.

JESSIE. You were twenty.

JOE. But remarkably mature for my age.

JESSIE. And I was eighteen and very *imm*ature. Not to mention "shy." I could help out backstage, but I would rather die than face an audience.

JOE. I couldn't stop looking at you. You were so cute. You still are.

JESSIE. That's what you told me. Actually, *you* didn't tell me. You were working with Eddie then. It was Eddie who told me you thought I was "cute."

JOE. Well, as long as you got the message, that's all that mattered.

JESSIE. That night, you and Eddie stole the show.

JOE. It was actually the first time I said to myself, "Hey, maybe I can make a living doing this—making people laugh."

JESSIE. And that was the night I began to fall in love with you.

JOE. (*trying to lighten the mood*) So a good time was had by all.

JESSIE. Of course, when we started dating, my Mom and Dad weren't very happy about it.

JOE. That's putting it mildly!

JESSIE. And when I told them we were getting married... I'm sure they prayed to every available Saint to stop us.

JOE. But we *did* get married.

JESSIE. Well, like I always say, "You can never find a Saint when you *need* one."

JOE. (*yawning, but making a mental note*) I like that line. I've got to remember it.

JESSIE. The first few years were really tough—for both of us.

JOE. I thought you loved being a waitress!

JESSIE. Not as much as *you* loved working on a loading dock.

JOE. Oh, my aching back!

JESSIE. But we had lots of fun, too, didn't we?

JOE. We sure did. We had each other. And we had Manhattan. Never mind "the Bronx and Staten Island, too."

JESSIE. And let us not forget our charming "walk-up" studio apartment— on the fourth floor of a West Side brownstone.

JOE. Climbing those stairs was great exercise!

JESSIE. And when you think of it, half the time you weren't going *up*, you were going *down*.

JOE. And most important, if you looked out the corner of the kitchen window, and tilted your head slightly to one side, you could see a thin slice of the Hudson River—*between* the two buildings across the street.

JESSIE. So of course, it was listed as a "river-view apartment."

JOE. It pays to advertise.

(*A pause as they reminisce.*)

JESSIE. Then we both got lucky—at the same time.

JOE. You met Jennie at a party in the Village.

JESSIE. (*with mock snobbery*) And of course, she hired me immediately.

JOE. It turned out you were born to be a travel agent.

JESSIE. Well, I was always dreaming of going to Paris—and Vienna—and Tokyo—and just about everywhere I'd never been. So I could understand other people's dreams. And I enjoyed making them come true.

JOE. You were making money, too! Good money. Still are.

JESSIE. And then a few weeks later, *you* got lucky.

JOE. Yeah. Can you believe it! Jay Leno has a buddy who's trying out his act at that little comedy club in Pasadena. What the hell was the name of that place?

JESSIE. The...uh...Laugh Factory.

JOE. Right. So Leno sees Eddie and me *by accident*. And he loves us. Bam! We get a spot on the Tonight Show.

JESSIE. And he keeps inviting you back, I don't know how many times. And then everything starts coming up roses for you.

JOE. For *both* of us.

JESSIE. (*without enthusiasm, softly*) Yes, for both of us.

JOE. (*yawns*) Listen, Honey. Can we stroll down Memory Lane tomorrow? Believe me, I could use a good night's sleep.

JESSIE. Just hang in there for a few more minutes, okay?

JOE. Okay. But I still don't get the message.

JESSIE. You will. (*pause*) When you started out, the way you played it, you and Eddie were always "surprised" by life. You were like innocent kids and everyone took advantage of you. Then Eddie began to wise up, to fight back. But *you* were still the perfect fall guy. And little by little, *he* also started taking advantage of you.

JOE. That's kind of a tradition. The straight man is a nice guy who can't control the funny guy. You can play that a lot of different ways.

JESSIE. After a while, it didn't seem to me like you were *playing*.

JOE. What do you mean?

JESSIE. Eddie kept getting nastier and nastier. He didn't just trick you and make fun of you, he insulted you. He told the audience what a fool you were. And what a fool you married.

JOE. It was just a routine. It's nothing to get upset about.

JESSIE. Then *I* became Target Number One. I couldn't even go to your shows any more. It was too embarrassing. My Mom and Dad were furious.

JOE. Okay, maybe we *did* overdo it a little.

JESSIE. No "maybe" about it.

JOE. But I dropped Eddie from the act, didn't I?

JESSIE. Finally. *Finally*! It took way too long.

JOE. Jessie, I didn't know how hurt you felt. I thought you stopped coming to the shows because maybe you were busy at work. Or just tired of seeing us. You never said anything. Why didn't you say something?

JESSIE. You're right. I *should* have told you.

JOE. I never wanted to hurt you.

JESSIE. Then you started working with Lola. And I really enjoyed the new act.

JOE. (*pleased that she's pleased*) Yeah. She's funny in a different way. Glamorous. Sexy. "Whatever Lola wants, Lola gets…"

JESSIE. You work very well with her. You're the Saint and she's the Sinner.

JOE. See, you *can* find a Saint when you need one!

JESSIE. (*not enjoying the joke*) But the new act has begun to change, too. A few months ago, Lola started talking about *me*. About me pressuring you to start a family.

JOE. Well, I was just…

JESSIE. That's not fair.

JOE. Jessie! Listen to what you're saying! For God's sake, Eddie and Lola are *dummies!*

JESSIE. But *I'm* not! When they talk, it's *your* voice I'm hearing. Eddie wasn't angry at me. You were. When Lola makes fun of me for wanting a child, it's *you* making fun of me.

JOE. (*lamely*) It's just a routine.

JESSIE. Joe, can't you see what you're doing? You're always hiding behind them. You're the good guy. The good husband. And they do all the dirty work for you. That has to stop. If you're upset with me, or angry, or you feel pressured, I don't want to hear Eddie or Lola bitching about it. *You* have to talk to me about it. Face to face. Joe, I love you.

JOE. I know you do.

JESSIE. Do you still love *me?*

JOE. Of course I do.

JESSIE. We can't keep going down this road. I want us to be happy, to enjoy our lives together.

JOE. So do I.

JESSIE. Then we have to start facing our *problems* together. Talking about them. Solving them. Together. Can we do that? Can *you?*

JOE. I know I've never been good at sharing my feelings. I don't know how. Where would I even start?

JESSIE. I'll help you, sweetheart. One step at a time.

JOE. I'm so sorry, Jess.

JESSIE. Don't worry. I'll be there for you.

JOE. I'm counting on you.

JESSIE. I know that.

JOE. I need you, Honey.

JESSIE. We'll work on it, Joe—you and I.

JOE. You and I...

JESSIE. Together.

JOE. Together. (*pause, thoughtfully*) But what about my act? People love Lola because she's so nasty. That's what makes them laugh. That's what sells. She can't turn into Mary Poppins!

JESSIE. Hey, Joe, I'm not the only target in town. (*pause, then she has an inspiration*) You want to keep Lola mean? What about all those politicians that keep making fools of themselves? She can have a field day!

JOE. Yeah, that's...one way to go.

JESSIE. And politicians aren't the only ones. Just read the paper every morning. Plenty of material there.

JOE. You're right about that.

JESSIE. Hey, why not read the paper *with* her, as part of the act? That could be a great shtick.

JOE. Yeah, yeah. Jessie, what would I do without you?

JESSIE. (*sweetly*) I can't imagine...

JOE. Well, I guess I know *one* thing for sure: *I've* turned out to be the dummy!

STAG LIGHTS

CHARACTERS:
EMERY FIELDING, *the friendly, retiring lighthouse keeper, in his forties.*
JACOB CARTER, *the eager, incoming lighthouse keeper, in his twenties.*

THE TIME: *1930.*
THE PLACE: *The dining room of the lighthouse keeper's home, on an island off the coast of Maine.*

As the action begins, EMERY *and* JACOB *enter the dining room.*

EMERY. Sit down, Jacob. Please. There's no rush.

JACOB. (*fretting*) I know, I know. But the sooner I get everything unpacked, the better I'll feel.

EMERY. You can finish that later. For God's sake, *relax.*

JACOB. I've never been good at that. (*humorously but nervously*) Lighthouse keepers better *not* relax, eh?

EMERY. It's a beautiful, clear night, Jacob. Nothing to worry about. And I checked the light an hour ago. It's still *my* responsibility until I leave tomorrow afternoon. Tell you what: I'm going to pour you a nice *glass* of relaxation.

JACOB. You mean you've been brewing Moonshine here? Or does Al Capone keep you supplied?

EMERY. If you're suggesting I did something illegal, let me explain. (*feigning innocence*) A case of fine French Chardonnay washed ashore a few months ago. I was walking on the beach and (what do you know?) I found it.

JACOB. Manna from Heaven, huh?

EMERY. Maybe some kind Canadian, who thinks Prohibition is a damn fool idea, which it *is*, tossed that case of wine into the ocean.

JACOB. And did he imagine it would wind up *here*?

EMERY. Well, he's not only kind, he's smart. He knows that the ice-cold Labrador current will carry the wine south, right past our door. And keep it chilled, too!

JACOB. That's a pretty tall story, Emery. I don't think Elliot Ness would buy it.

EMERY. What the Feds don't know won't hurt them. (*raising his glass*) To Jacob Carter—the new lighthouse keeper on our island—on *your* island. Welcome! And good luck!

JACOB. (*raising his glass*) Thank you, Emery. (*drinks*) Mmm...Tasty. But I guess you know I'm no expert.

EMERY. Well, truthfully, neither am I. So, Jacob, tell me about yourself.

JACOB. Why does that matter to you? You're leaving.

EMERY. This *place* matters to me. I've given ten hard years of my life to it. And much more than that. I want to know all about the man who's taking over.

JACOB. You must have read my file.

EMERY. Just bare-bones, bureaucratic nonsense. Nothing about the *real* Jacob Carter.

JACOB. Okay. If that's your pleasure. I was born and grew up in Syracuse, New York. (*disparagingly*) Not a *bad* little city.

EMERY. But not a *good* little city?

JACOB. Boring. Like my family. My Dad was an accountant. Had his own firm. Made good money. Mom did the usual Mom stuff: cooking, baking, cleaning. She seemed to enjoy it. (*sarcastically*) They were "God-fearing" people.

EMERY. And you *don't* fear God?

JACOB. If there *is* a God—and the jury's still out—he doesn't care about us one way or the other. I think we're an experiment that went wrong, and he took off for another galaxy to try his luck again.

EMERY. No Heaven for the good guys? No Hell for the bad ones?

JACOB. When you die, you die. It's over. Period.

EMERY. Let's get back to your life story. Brothers? Sisters?

JACOB. An older brother, Jack. He was just like Dad. A number cruncher. Joined Dad's firm right after college. And there's my sister Emily, a couple of years younger than me. She married a guy whose father owns three or four hotels. So Em did all right for herself.

EMERY. What about *you*, Jacob? What did *you* do?

JACOB. After I dropped out of high school, I left home for good. I kept in touch but I never went back. I'm sure they don't miss me. They were probably *relieved*.

EMERY. Where'd you go?

JACOB. I hitched a ride on the "Hobo Express." You don't have to buy a ticket. Just hop on a freight car and get off whenever the fancy takes you.

EMERY. Sad to say, in hard times like these, lots of people are riding that train.

JACOB. Yeah, I had plenty of company. I went out to the Midwest. Ohio. Indiana. I'm pretty handy with machines—always was. I never had trouble finding work. You know, fixing cars or tractors. Odd jobs on a farm or shifts in a factory. Even pick-up work harvesting corn or wheat. You name it, likely I done it. I slept just about everywhere in my sleeping bag: barns, the back rooms of gas stations, park benches.

EMERY. Never settled anywhere?

JACOB. Nah.. I didn't want to be tied down. I've never needed anyone. Sure, there were girls along the way. But I wasn't looking for companionship.

EMERY. (*almost to himself*) You're still young.

JACOB. I finally got tired of wandering. But I wanted the right kind of job—a perfect fit.

EMERY. The Lighthouse Service.

JACOB. Yeah. I told them I wanted to work alone in the most isolated place they could find. I had no family. Wanted none. Wanted no help. I said I could do the job by myself.

EMERY. What we call a "stag light."

JACOB. Yeah, that's what I was looking for. A stag light. But that's not what they gave me. They sent me to North Carolina. I was the keeper's assistant. He had his family living with him—a wife and three kids. And there were houses—a little village—close by.

EMERY. But you learned the trade.

JACOB. There were lots of ships, lots of crazy weather. A good place to learn. But too many goddamn people!

EMERY. And when you heard I was leaving, you jumped at the chance to come here—to an island, an *isolated* island.

JACOB. It's perfect. Plenty of action—where a cold current meets a warm one. There'll be enough goddamn fog to keep me busy all year round.

EMERY. You're right about that.

JACOB. So, Emery, that's my story. I'm here to take over your stag light.

EMERY. This wasn't my stag light for the time I was here.

JACOB. You're alone, aren't you?

EMERY. I'm alone *now*. Let me refill your glass. You told me your story. Now I'll tell you mine.

JACOB. (*drinks some wine*) I think I could learn to like this stuff. My thanks to that kind Canadian!

EMERY. I was a lot like you. Always a loner. Never a joiner. I grew up on a farm in Pennsylvania. A dairy farm.

JACOB. So you're a hayseed, huh?

EMERY. Yep. My folks were decent, hardworking people. But they never showed me much affection. I guess they couldn't help it. My mother kept birthing weak babies, babies that died. I was the only strong one in the litter. The only one who survived.

JACOB. Didn't that make you special for them?

EMERY. No, it didn't. Maybe they were afraid that if they cared about me too much, if they loved me too much, *I* would die, too. But they lost me anyway. After high school, I worked on the farm for a few years. There was talk about me marrying one of the local girls but that was *her* idea, not mine. One day, I told my folks I was leaving. It seemed like they expected it, like they knew it *had* to be.

JACOB. Where'd you go?

EMERY. Philadelphia.

JACOB. A big city like that? All those people?

EMERY. You ever live in a big city? Not a little burg like Syracuse. Sure, Philadelphia is crowded but, if you know how, you can be alone in the crowd. You know the old riddle: Where do you hide an egg?

JACOB. I don't know that one.

EMERY. You hide it in a chicken coop, with all the *other* eggs. It's the same in a big city like Philadelphia. Where do you hide yourself? In a crowd of a million people. It's easy. Take my word for it.

JACOB. If you say so.

EMERY. I got a night job stacking shelves in a supermarket. I lived a couple of blocks away. Room and board with an old lady. She had a basement to rent in a house that was even older than *she* was. But you know what made it perfect? She was deaf and she was too vain to wear a hearing aid.

JACOB. So you didn't have to talk to her!

EMERY. And I didn't see much of her. I slept during the day. Worked six nights a week. Made most of my own meals. Ate with her on Sundays, after she came back from church. We didn't talk much, but I smiled and nodded and that was enough for her.

JACOB. How long were you in Philly?

EMERY. A year or so. Then I read a story in the paper about a lighthouse keeper. What he did. The kind of life he led.

JACOB. Sounded good, huh?

EMERY. It was what I was looking for. What I needed. And after I joined, I did what you did: I asked for a stag light.

JACOB. Did you get it?

EMERY. No. My first job was like yours. It was on the Florida coast. I was there for almost five years. My second assignment, in Georgia, was just about the same. Another four years and no stag light yet.

JACOB. Was this place next?

EMERY. Nope. Rhode Island was, and it was the *opposite* of what I wanted. I had an assistant who was married. They had a kid. They lived in a cottage near the lighthouse. And there was a town within walking distance, less than a mile away. But I figured I'd be patient and make the best of it until something better turned up.

JACOB. I know the feeling.

EMERY. Then something *did* turn up, something I never expected. (*pause*) I used to walk to the library in town, and pick up some books. Mysteries, usually. I liked those.

JACOB. I can never wait till the end to find out who did it. I always look!

EMERY. I can believe that. Anyway, I got a little tired of mysteries, so I asked the librarian for some suggestions, her recommendations. (*thoughtfully, remembering*) Her name was Joanna. She was a few years younger than me. Almost as tall. Very slim. An ordinary-looking woman. Not someone who turned heads. She spoke softly, slowly, as if she was careful about picking the right words. She said she could recommend some books, but they might not be easy reading. "You may have to work hard to understand them," she said. "But you're used to hard work, aren't you?"

JACOB. I would have told her to forget it!

EMERY. I almost did. But for some reason, I didn't. And she gave me a book to read. "Mutiny on the Bounty." It was about a real mutiny that happened a long time ago on an English ship. It was a good story. She said she figured a lighthouse keeper would enjoy a book like that. A sea story.

JACOB. Was it hard to understand?

EMERY. No. And I told her so.

JACOB. Was she disappointed?

EMERY. No. She gave me this big smile and said she was "starting me off slowly."

JACOB. What did she mean, "starting you off"?

EMERY. She was going to teach me—educate me.

JACOB. Why would she do that?

EMERY. I guess she liked me...liked being with me. When I was reading one of those books, we would talk about it. And she would help me dig deeper, help me understand more.

JACOB. Sounds kinda boring.

EMERY. It wasn't. She kept taking me to new places, new...*worlds*. (*pause*) And the Joanna I'd gotten to know wasn't so ordinary-looking anymore— she was beautiful. I loved to look at her, to listen to her soft voice.

JACOB. Oh, brother! You were a goner!

EMERY. You're right. I fell in love with her. *Loving* was a new feeling for me. And it felt good. Best of all, she said she loved me, too. I asked her to marry me.

JACOB. Going, going, gone!

EMERY. (*absorbed in his memories*) She didn't say "yes" right away. She said if I wanted children, she couldn't give them to me. She'd had an operation when she was a teenager: she couldn't have children. I said that didn't matter. I said that all I wanted—all I would *ever* want—was her. I felt my luck was changing and, a few months after we got married, I finally got assigned here. I applied for this place more than a year before I met Joanna. This was going to be (at last!) my stag light. But instead, it became *our* world—Joanna's and mine. A perfect world.

JACOB. It's a tough life for a woman like her, isn't it?

EMERY. At first, I worried about that, too. But she surprised me. She never complained. She seemed to enjoy the way we lived. Some nights— the worst nights... Heavy fog. Bitter-cold winds. The sea roaring as if it was angry at us. The fog horn blasting away every 15 seconds. I'd be up and down in the tower, up and down. It would be I-don't-know-how-many-hours before it cleared. And she'd have a bowl of clam chowder, piping hot, waiting for me. Or beef stew. And big, thick slabs of buttered bread. And a pot of hot coffee. And with her long, slim fingers she'd try to squeeze the tightness out of my neck and back. And sometimes, while she was comforting me, she would be reciting a poem—practically *singing* it to me.

JACOB. A poem?

EMERY. She often did that. Not just when there were storms. It could be any time. She knew a lot of poems. I didn't always understand the words, but because of the way she *said* them, I could understand what they meant. It was like listening to music. (*several beats while* EMERY *remembers*) It was a hard life we shared. And yet the sharing made it a *good* life. Then, last April, after almost nine years together, it suddenly was over. I should have known...

JACOB. Known *what*?

EMERY. You said it's a tough life for a woman like her. You're right. She gave me strength but it cost her too much. It wore her down. (*bitterly*) I should have seen it... I'll never forgive myself. Never.

JACOB. (*after a long, awkward silence*) What happened?

EMERY. One morning, a sunny Spring morning, a beautiful morning, we were having breakfast. Joanna said she hadn't slept well. She said she needed to take a nap and would I wake her in an hour or so? I told her "of course" and said she could sleep longer than that, if she wanted to. I wish I had never said that. (*drinks wine*) She looked so tired, I let *two* hours go by before I went into the bedroom to wake her. I...couldn't wake her. She... never woke up.

JACOB. (*softly, embarrassed*) Sorry.

EMERY. (*as if to himself*) Most of my life, I've been alone but I was never lonely. Now, and from now on, I always *will* be. And it was my fault.

(*A long pause*)

JACOB. (*reflecting on "what he's learned"*) You know, Emery, I still think a stag light is the right place—the best place for *me*. I don't need anything more. I don't need love.

EMERY. That's what I used to think, too. But it isn't true, Jacob. Loving someone and being loved—that's the best thing.

JACOB. Even if you lose her?

EMERY. Even if you lose her.

JACOB. (*after a beat*) Thanks for the wine, Emery. And the life story. But I should unpack my bags now.

EMERY. Okay. We'll go over the log books and the charts in the morning. And all the gear. But I'm sure there's nothing here you haven't seen before. I'll sleep on the couch.

JACOB. Where's your next hitch?

EMERY. There *isn't* any next hitch. I'm leaving the Service. I'm going to see my Aunt Marian. She's a widow, all alone. She lives in New York, a few miles from Utica.

JACOB. Just the kind of place I ran away from! But I forgot: you're a hayseed at heart.

EMERY. I called her a few months ago. She's the only family I've got left. She owns a general store up there. Needs some help, she says.

JACOB. *You*, a storekeeper?

EMERY. It's a start.

JACOB. You're welcome to it. See you in the morning.

EMERY. Good night, Jacob. (*after* JACOB *leaves*; *tenderly*) This is my last night here, my love. My last night. Jacob is very young, hurting the way I was hurting when I met you. And he's very sure about everything. The way *I* was. And he's just as wrong as I was. He doesn't know how loving changes who you are. How being loved makes you better than you thought you could be. I hope he finds out. (*softly*) Good night, Joanna. And sweet dreams forever.

STUCK ON YOU

CHARACTERS:
JOSHUA, *a frustrated actor, about 27 years old.*
MARTHA, *a fortune-teller, outgoing, friendly, about 50 years old.*

THE TIME: *Mid-morning.*
THE PLACE: *An elevator on the ground floor of a 60-story building.*

As the action begins, MARTHA is running to reach the elevator before the door closes.

MARTHA. (*breathlessly*) Hold the elevator! Please! (*JOSHUA reaches out to hold the door.*) Thank you. You're a real gentleman.

JOSHUA. (*Shrugs. His mind is elsewhere. He isn't really paying attention to her. Mumbling under his breath*) A real gentleman... That's me.

MARTHA. Would you press "42" for me? Thanks. (*pause*) Oh, I see you're going all the way to the top! The 60th floor! What's up there?

JOSHUA. (*very dramatically*) What's up there? (*dramatic pause*) Samara.

MARTHA. That sounds like one of those Japanese techie companies. Laptops. Cell phones.

JOSHUA. (*indifferently, distractedly*) Does it?

MARTHA. I'll bet you're a—what do they call it nowadays?--a *geek*?

JOSHUA. (*shakes his head*) Never *was*... Never *will* be...

(*There's a loud buzzing sound and the elevator stops suddenly between floors, with a shake.*)

MARTHA. (*amused, rather than worried*) Look at that! We're stuck!

JOSHUA. (*laughing bitterly, speaking softly to himself*) I can't even get *this* right! The final indignity.

MARTHA. (*unworried, cheerfully optimistic*) We'll probably start again in a minute or two. The lights didn't go out, so it's no big deal. (JOSHUA *doesn't respond.*) You know, in the movies, whenever people get stuck in an elevator, one of them usually turns out to be a murderer—or the Devil. (*smiling*) Should I be worried?

JOSHUA. (*sullenly, offhandedly*) This isn't a movie. You're perfectly safe.

MARTHA. (*half seriously*) Well... Maybe *not*. Because what I *really* worry about is that the cable—you know, the one pulling us up—could break and *bam!*... (*with a sly smile*) we're *shafted*.

JOSHUA. (*ignoring the play on words, still gloomy*) You don't have to worry about that, either. When he invented his elevator, Mr. Otis took care of that. He threw in a gadget that *stops* it from falling if the cable breaks.

MARTHA. So you looked it up, huh? I guess *you've* worried about that, too.

JOSHUA. (*sourly*) I didn't have to look it up. The father of my best friend— or should I say, the father of that miserable *rat* of an *ex*-friend—owns a company that *installs* elevators. So I know a lot about them. Maybe they installed *this* one. Ha! That would be the icing on the cake.

MARTHA. (*trying to steer him to a safer topic*) Ummm... What you said before—that you were going to "Samara?" I never heard of it.

JOSHUA. (*dramatically, as if he were performing a soliloquy*) Ah, well... A young prince thought he saw Death walking in the marketplace. Afraid that Death had come for *him*, he rushed back to the palace, told one of his servants what he'd seen, and fled to another town far away, a town called Samara. The servant, who didn't believe the prince's story, went to the marketplace. And, sure enough...there was Death. He told Death why the prince had run away. And Death said, "He was wrong. I didn't come for him *today*. But *tomorrow*...we have an appointment in Samara."

MARTHA. (*thinking about the story*) So... I still don't get it. (*then, realizing what his story means*) Ohhh... No... Are you going up there to...?

VOICE. (*interrupting, over the Public Address system*) Folks, this is Janet Goldman, the building manager. Please stay calm. We're working as fast as we can and I promise you, we'll have you moving in no time. I'll keep you posted on our progress. So, just try to stay calm.

MARTHA. (*ignoring the interruption*) Never mind the *prince*... Let's talk about *you*. I can tell you're not happy. Maybe it would help to talk to *me* about it. I'm a stranger. We'll probably never meet again. And maybe you'll feel better if you just get it off your chest.

JOSHUA. (*hesitating*) I don't know...

MARTHA. (*trying to be reassuring*) Even if I *can't* solve your problem—

JOSHUA. You definitely *can't*...

MARTHA. (*shrugging*) Well...what *else* have we got to do?

JOSHUA. (*sighs, speaks softly, to himself*) What's bothering me...? (*He still hesitates.*)

MARTHA. (*trying to break the ice*) My name is Martha. What's *yours*?

JOSHUA. Joshua.

MARTHA. Joshua, I'm listening. Talk to me.

JOSHUA. (*nods*) Okay. Why not? Let's start with my "career." I'm an actor. I've got good credentials: an MFA from Yale Drama School. I'm talented. (Take my word for it.) I'm not bad-looking. But so far—and I'm talking about the last *four* years—all I've done is *bit* parts—on the stage, Off Broadway—but mostly on TV. A line or two, if I'm lucky. Nothing more. A couple of times, I've been murdered on "Law and Order." It's dark. I hear a noise behind me. I turn around and scream and I'm shot or stabbed or decapitated. And then, for an encore, I'm laid out, naked, under a sheet, so the Medical Examiner can take a closer look at the damages. Not exactly "King Lear." (*pause*) But *every* time I audition for a part that *matters*, I don't get it.

MARTHA. Do you know *why*? You *must* know why.

JOSHUA. (*exasperated*) It's never for the same reason! (*He uses a variety of voices for each rejection.*) "You're too tall. You'll make the leading man look like a shrimp." "You're too short. She'll look like your *mother*, not your wife." "You're too old." "Too young." "Too handsome." "Too ugly." (*pause*) And my all-time favorite: "You're just not *right* for the part."

MARTHA. (*as if she's remembering something*) You know, come to think of it, I may have seen you on TV. You look familiar.

JOSHUA. (*with a sad smile*) Yes, I'm sure you *have* seen me. *Millions* of people have. I'm dressed up in a blue jump suit and a little hat with a bell on it. Ding dong! I'm a freaking *elf!* Elvis, the Mushy-Tushy Toilet Paper Elf. And I'm cuter than shit. (How appropriate!) I tell the viewing audience, in my whining little voice: "*Go* in comfort—with Mushy-Tushy Toilet Tissues—softer than a Cloud. Put that comfort *behind* you." (*in his own voice*) I guess I aced *that* freaking audition!

MARTHA. Okay, Joshua, it's not Shakespeare, but it's a *job*. I'll bet you're getting paid well. And it's a start, isn't it? Listen, you're still very young. Give it some time. I'm sure you'll get plenty of chances. I can understand how discouraging it is. But you can't give up and...for *God's* sake!...you can't...you *mustn't* go to the "*60th floor*." That's not the answer.

JOSHUA. (*sadly*) Oh, it isn't just my so-called career. That's not the worst of it.

MARTHA. (*now obviously dedicated to helping* JOSHUA) Look, I'm still here. I'm still listening. Talk to me.

JOSHUA. (*suspicion dawning*) "Talk to me"? Hey, what's all this "talk to me" crap? Are you a shrink or something—looking for new business?

MARTHA. (*smiles*) No, I'm *not* a shrink. But I *am* used to talking to people about their problems. Sometimes, even helping to *solve* them. I'm... (*she searches for the right word*) We're called a lot of things: "mediums," "psychics"... but...

JOSHUA. (*laughs*) You're a *fortune teller*? What a freaking racket *that* is! Tea leaves? Crystal balls? Spirits banging on the table? That's worse than selling toilet paper!

MARTHA. (*without taking offense*) Not the way *I* do it.

JOSHUA. Come on, Martha. Get real. You're not going to tell me you can see the future? That you *knew* we were going to get stuck in this elevator?

MARTHA. Of course not. I can't see the future. And the Tarot cards and the tea leaves, that's all window dressing, make believe. My clients *expect* it, and I don't disappoint them. And most of it is harmless. But what's important for *me* is that sometimes, I *can* help people. Not by telling them what their future *will* be—but by helping them decide what their future *could* be.

JOSHUA. And you think you've got the right to do that? That takes a lot of nerve.

MARTHA. It may sound like that, but...

VOICE. (*interrupting, on the Public Address system*) This is the Building Manager again. The repairman says the elevator will be back in service in ten or fifteen minutes. (*optimistically*) So *hang* in there—(*realizing that's the wrong way to say it*)—uh, I mean, please be patient. Thank you.

JOSHUA. (*distracted from his own problems*) You think it's right for you to do that? Give people advice like that? People you don't even know?

MARTHA. (*patiently, not defensively*) Listen, Joshua. I've always been very good at "reading" people. Even when I was young. I guess you could call it a "gift." It's not just what people *say*. It's maybe what they *don't* say. Or the *way* they say it. I can usually *sense* what they *really* mean—what they really *want*.

JOSHUA. (*sarcastically*) And that "magical power" is your key to success, huh?

MARTHA. (*patiently*) There's nothing "magical" about it. And when someone tells me about what she's afraid of, or what's gone wrong with her life, I understand where she's coming from. Because, believe me, I've been there. I know what life can throw at you. I had a wonderful marriage, but my husband died when he was only forty. I feel that loss—that emptiness— every day.

JOSHUA. Sorry. That's a bummer.

MARTHA. And my daughter—smart, successful—had a *terrible* marriage... to a real loser.

JOSHUA. (*grudgingly, sympathetically*) Okay, okay. So you've had your problems, too.

MARTHA. And...you said that I hadn't heard the *worst* of *yours*.

JOSHUA. (*a little less gloomy because of* MARTHA's *revelations*) My girlfriend Amy... (*in a sing-song style*) "Once in love with Amy—*always* in love with Amy"... I thought it was going to be like that for us. That my search was over. That it would "always" be Amy. That we were soul mates. (*warming to the topic*) And then Martin...

MARTHA. The elevator tycoon's son?

JOSHUA. Yeah. My *supposed* best friend...behind my *back*...*stole* her from me.

MARTHA. (*after a pause*) You know, Joshua, if you were a client of mine...

JOSHUA. No way!

MARTHA. (*laughs*) But just for argument's sake. You know what I would tell you? Martin didn't *steal* Amy. She's not something you *owned*. She's a *person*—and *she* decided that she'd rather be *Martin's* girlfriend. That happens. And it's not the end of the world, although it seems like that now.

JOSHUA. But she was *perfect*.

MARTHA. Do you really think *anybody* is perfect? Are *you* perfect? (*pause*) Joshua, this isn't a *play*, where everything is settled before the curtain falls. Life keeps going on. Some of it is good and some of it *isn't*. (*smiling*) And we all end up in Samara one of these days. But you've got plenty of time. Don't be in such a rush to get there.

JOSHUA. (*beginning to be won over*) Is that what your crystal ball says?

MARTHA. (*touching her head, pretending to see the future*) Actually, I'm receiving another message: It's my daughter Stacey. She's up on the 42nd floor. (*proudly*) She's the marketing manager for an international cable network. I'm meeting her for lunch. (*looking up at the ceiling of the elevator*) And there seems to be a *third* chair at the table. An *empty* chair. Why don't you join us?

JOSHUA. (*tentatively*) Well, I don't know...

MARTHA. Joshua, there's *nothing* for you on the 60th floor. Maybe there's *something* for you on the 42nd.

(*There's a loud buzz as the elevator starts again.*)

VOICE. (*on Public Address system*) We're back in business! Thank you for your patience.

MARTHA. (*smiles*) You know, come to think of it, you and Stacey actually have a lot in common. She's always been a bit of a *drama queen*!

PROFESSOR SUNSHINE

CHARACTERS:
AMELIA HARPER, *a timid young woman.*
MICHAEL SCHEIN (*pronounced* "Shine"), *an escaped fugitive, in his fifties.*

THE TIME: *The present.*
THE PLACE: *The kitchen of a suburban house.*

AMELIA HARPER. (*speaking directly to the audience*) I'd like to tell you what happened, while it's still fresh in my mind. Because memory can be tricky. You know....You get together with people. Friends or family. You start talking about somebody's wedding... or birthday party... or something. You think you remember it pretty well. But your memory is different from theirs. Are you wrong? You don't think so. But they don't think they're wrong, either. Maybe you're *both* wrong. (*pause*) Anyway, I'm going to tell you about something that happened just a few days ago. I'm the only one who'll remember it, so you'll have to take my word for it. Okay?

This place—this house—is just too big for me. I didn't want it. But my mother wouldn't let me give it up. She was my divorce lawyer. She's good at it. *Very* good. She said, "We're gonna *screw* Steve." (He's my ex.) She said, (*imitating her mother's nasty expression*) "You'll get the house. And as much alimony as I can squeeze out of him." And she *squeezed* him like an orange. (*sighs*) So I got this house. Out in the woods. Which I *didn't* want. It's hard enough living alone. But there's four acres of woods around me (and it might as well be a *thousand*). It's scary out here. Yes, I admit it. I'm not the bravest person in the world. A lot of things scare me. I keep the alarm on all the time. I can tell you this. My mother scared the hell out of *Steve*. And he doesn't scare easily.

Last Sunday morning I was at the kitchen table, eating breakfast. Trying to do some work. I brought home a manuscript I was editing—a biography of Emily Dickinson. It wasn't very good. It was about her loneliness. Not much about her *poems*. Gossip. That's what people want to read these days. It levels the playing field. They say, "Emily Dickinson may have been a great poet, but she was *crazy*." I guess that's a comfort to some people. They may not have any *talent*...but at least they aren't crazy. Anyway, the manuscript was sitting on the table, waiting. Like Emily? Like me? But I kept looking out the window at the leaves floating down. (*slowly, wistfully*) Red. Yellow. Gold. Summer dying...slowly. (*sighs*) The last thing I wanted to do was read another manuscript. But I didn't feel like doing anything else. I watched a pair of squirrels chasing each other, hopping from trunk to trunk, branch to branch. Are they fighting? Or flirting? I guess only squirrels can tell the difference. They move so fast, it's amazing they don't fall, they don't get hurt. It must feel great to be that *sure* of yourself... I decided to take a break. A drive would be good, a change of scene. I turned off the alarm and pushed the garage door button... And there he was...

(MICHAEL SCHEIN *is holding a revolver, pointing it at* AMELIA. *His clothes are wrinkled and dirty. His hair is disheveled.*)

SCHEIN. Stop right there!

AMELIA. Oh, God...

SCHEIN. Look at me!

AMELIA. What do you want?

SCHEIN. I said "Look at me"!

AMELIA. (*terrified*) I'm looking at you!

SCHEIN. We're going back into the house.

AMELIA. (*almost whispering*) Into the house...

SCHEIN. I don't want to hurt you. Do what I say and I won't hurt you.

AMELIA. (*trying and failing to calm down*) What—what do you want?

SCHEIN. Is anybody else home?

AMELIA. No. No. I—I live alone.

SCHEIN. Alone? Are you sure? You're not lying to me?

AMELIA. I'm *not* lying. I *swear*. I live alone. What do you want?

SCHEIN. (*He sits at the kitchen table, exhausted.*) What do I *want*? God only knows. (*He gestures with the revolver.*) Sit down. You're not going anywhere. (*pause*) What *do* I want? A new lease on life? A new identity? Plastic surgery, maybe. I don't suppose you're a plastic surgeon.

AMELIA. No, I'm not. I'm—an editor.

SCHEIN. (*shakes his head, disgusted*) Just my luck. A clueless intellectual. Welcome to the club. (*more softly*) I'm hungry. And thirsty.

AMELIA. (*anxiously, trying to be cooperative*) I could—I don't know—cook something.

SCHEIN. I've been sleeping in the woods. I don't need a gourmet meal.

AMELIA. A sandwich. I could make you a sandwich. Roast beef? And cheese. Swiss cheese?

SCHEIN. *Two* sandwiches. You can do that, right? And something to drink. Anything will do.

AMELIA. Orange juice?

SCHEIN. Give me the container. (*She gets the container from the refrigerator and hands it to him. He drinks the juice as he watches her prepare the sandwiches.*) Why such a big house?

AMELIA. I was married. (*bitterly*) This was *our* house.

SCHEIN. Your "dream house?"

AMELIA. No. My husband wanted to live here. *I* never did.

SCHEIN. But you lived here anyway.

AMELIA. Yes, we did.

SCHEIN. And you argued endlessly about it?

AMELIA. No, not much.

SCHEIN. Why not? You got the right to vote a long time ago.

AMELIA. (*softly*) I don't argue. I never argue.

SCHEIN. Why the hell not?

AMELIA. Because I always lose.

(*She puts the food down on the table.*)

SCHEIN. Sit down. (*He gestures with the revolver toward the chair opposite him.*) Right there. (*He puts the revolver down on the table, the barrel still pointing at AMELIA. She watches him eat and drink.*) What's your name?

AMELIA. Amelia.

SCHEIN. So you never argue, Amelia? That's a bad attitude.

AMELIA. (*agreeing, afraid to contradict him*) Yes, I guess you could say that.

SCHEIN. What happened to your husband? Is he lost in the woods?

AMELIA. (*calming down a little as she starts thinking about her life*) We got divorced. Six months ago.

SCHEIN. And you kept the house to spite him?

AMELIA. My mother... She was my divorce lawyer.

SCHEIN. And she hates his guts, of course.

AMELIA. She made sure I got the house. And plenty of alimony.

SCHEIN. And he was hung out to dry.

AMELIA. (*bitterly*) Don't worry about him. He can afford it.

SCHEIN. So he's a rich guy?

AMELIA. (*calmer now*) He sells real estate. He always seems to make money.... Even in bad times.

SCHEIN. I know the type. I never had the knack. My brother-in-law is an ignorant man. Has the personality of a mushroom. But he knows how to make money. It's always been a mystery to me.

AMELIA. To me, too.

SCHEIN. How long were you married?

AMELIA. Five years.

SCHEIN. I was married for *twenty* years. You didn't have kids?

AMELIA. He said he wasn't ready.

SCHEIN. His sperm wasn't ripe yet?

AMELIA. He didn't explain.

SCHEIN. Were *you* ready?

AMELIA. I guess so. I think so.

SCHEIN. He sounds like an asshole. (*softly*) Children can change your life. A child can be...(*dismissing the thought*) How was the sex?

AMELIA. (*Her anger at her ex-husband has taken the edge off her fear.*) I don't know. It was all right.

SCHEIN. In other words, it was terrible.

AMELIA. Not always. But it was mostly about *his* pleasure. Not mine.

SCHEIN. A genuine, first-rate asshole.

AMELIA. (*with a touch of boldness*) And he wasn't very good at it.

SCHEIN. Did you ever tell him that?

AMELIA. No, but I wish I had.

SCHEIN. Right. You don't argue. But I'm sure he knew it. Even genuine assholes know things like that.

AMELIA. He was an immoral bastard, too.

SCHEIN. In business, you mean?

AMELIA. In everything he did...and said. In *everything*.

SCHEIN. Deep down, this may be the *real* Amelia. *Angry*. Not afraid.

AMELIA. I'm afraid of *you*.

SCHEIN. So am I. I never used to be. It shows you: you never really know who you are. Give me a cup of coffee.

AMELIA. It's cold. I'll warm it up in the microwave.

SCHEIN. Okay. (*pause*) I slept in the woods last night. Quite an experience.

AMELIA. I can imagine... It must have been...

SCHEIN. I couldn't believe how cold it was. I'm not exactly the forest ranger type. I kept hearing animals moving around. I didn't know what the hell they were... Deer maybe?

AMELIA. There *are* lots of deer out there.

SCHEIN. I was afraid. And then I thought, "Hey, I'm one of them. A target. On the run."

AMELIA. (*reminded of her fear*) On the run?

SCHEIN. (*ignoring her question*) After a while, I stopped feeling the cold. I fell asleep. (*She gives him coffee. He drinks some.*) I had a nightmare. A beautiful young girl was falling. I reached out for her. I tried to hold onto her, but I couldn't. She disappeared into the darkness. I could hear her screaming, "Help me! Help me!" I couldn't save her. (*pause*) Do you have something sweet? Cake? Candy?

AMELIA. Chocolate chip cookies? Is that okay?

(*He nods. She brings him the box of cookies and sits down again. He picks up the revolver. He doesn't point it at* AMELIA. *He holds it in his hand and studies it.*)

SCHEIN. Amazing invention, isn't it? We humans are clever at that sort of thing. A little bundle of steel. Streamlined. Shiny. Almost a work of art. And it can erase a life—a *lifetime*—in a split second. I can vouch for that. (*He eats a cookie.*) You think of yourself as civilized. "I'd never do *that*"... Maybe not. But don't count on it. Hey, don't worry. I won't be here long. Just passing through. Some food. A little rest.

AMELIA. If you need money... I don't have much, but...

SCHEIN. I don't need your money. It won't help. (*He studies* AMELIA *for a moment.*) So you're not a teacher? You look like my third-grade teacher.

AMELIA. I told you. I work for a publisher. I'm an editor.

SCHEIN. Yes, you told me. (*He picks up the manuscript on the table, riffles through it. Reads a fragment here and there. He puts it down again.*) I never liked Emily Dickinson's poems. Too fragile. Wispy, like smoke. What about you? You like her work?

AMELIA. In small doses.

SCHEIN. I prefer e.e. cummings. Funny. Sexy. Strong stuff. (*He smiles.*) You can't figure me out, huh? Well... Would you believe I was a teacher. A college prof, actually. And good at it.

AMELIA. (*surprised, almost forgetting her fear*) What did you teach?

SCHEIN. English Lit. But that was in another world. (*changing the subject*) I want to know more about *you*. Tell me about yourself. Your family.

AMELIA. I told you. My mother is a divorce lawyer.

SCHEIN. Did she divorce your father?

AMELIA. No. He's a chemist. Works for a drug company.

SCHEIN. That's an evil business, isn't it?

AMELIA. Evil? You really think so?

SCHEIN. Sure I do. They don't look for cures. Bad for the bottom line. They like *remedies*. Stuff you have to keep taking for years, just to stay alive.

AMELIA. I never thought of it that way.

SCHEIN. Do you have any brothers or sisters?

AMELIA. (*Her resentment of her family is apparent.*) A sister. She's the local TV news anchor. Very successful. My whole family is.

SCHEIN. Sounds like a hell of a line-up.

AMELIA. My mother calls me the "runt of the litter." As if that's a *joke*, not an *insult*.

SCHEIN. She doesn't think you match up to them?

AMELIA. And she keeps reminding me of that, over and over.

SCHEIN. And you let her do that?

AMELIA. (*wearily*) She wears me down.

SCHEIN. What the hell does *that* mean?

AMELIA. I'm not as strong as her. As *any* of them.

SCHEIN. Like I said: bad attitude. You've got to learn to argue. Wear *them* down.

AMELIA. (*shrugs*) Do you want more coffee?

SCHEIN. Yes. (*She pours him another cup.*) Alas, poor Amelia. Another good person bites the dust. Happens all the time.

AMELIA. I hardly notice it any more. It's like a habit. Hard to break.

SCHEIN. I know what you mean. You settle into a groove. You get comfortable. Doesn't matter whether it's good or bad. It's you.

AMELIA. Yes. That's what it's like.

SCHEIN. I had a *good* groove. Very good. Thought it was the real thing. Thought God was on my side.

AMELIA. That's a comforting thought.

SCHEIN. My parents. They said, "Aim for the stars." I did.

AMELIA. You believed in yourself.

SCHEIN. With a vengeance. I was a little smart-ass. Too smart for my own good.

AMELIA. But it worked for you?

SCHEIN. Oh, yeah. I knocked them out in school. Scholarship kid. Finished my undergrad work in three years. Had a Ph.D. in no time at all. I was the youngest full professor in the department when I met a wonderful girl and married her.

AMELIA. You were lucky.

SCHEIN. That's all it was. Luck. I wasn't God's favorite. He had nothing to do with it. I was just lucky.

AMELIA. What's wrong with that?

SCHEIN. Your luck can change.

AMELIA. *I* could use a little luck. If I could...

(*She doesn't finish the sentence.*)

SCHEIN. What were you going to say? Tell me.

AMELIA. If I could do what I want to do...

SCHEIN. And what's that?

AMELIA. I want to stop editing other people's work. I want to write my *own*.

SCHEIN. Why don't you?

AMELIA. They don't think I have enough talent.

SCHEIN. "They?" Your illustrious family. What do *you* think?

AMELIA. I don't know. I'm not sure.

SCHEIN. Come on, Amelia. What do you think?

AMELIA. (*cautiously*) I have talent. I just don't know how much.

SCHEIN. Don't listen to *them*. Screw them.

AMELIA. My mother said, "You have to get a real job. Write in your spare time."

SCHEIN. What a vote of confidence. Screw her, too.

AMELIA. I wish....

SCHEIN. I know, I know. She wears you down.

AMELIA. (*almost mocking herself*) Yes, she wears me down.

SCHEIN. You know what? That's a lousy excuse.

AMELIA. If I had my choice, I would sell this house and move to Boston. And write. I love Boston.

SCHEIN. Amelia, believe me, you *have* a choice.

AMELIA. I suppose I *do*.

SCHEIN. And you also have a problem. Everybody wears you down.

AMELIA. It sounds pretty silly, when you say it that way.

SCHEIN. Listen, everybody makes mistakes. *I* made the wrong choices, too. (*He pauses, looks down at the revolver, touches it with his fingertips, caresses it.*) My wife's name was Margery. I called her Margery Daw. (*sings*) "See-saw, Margery Daw." She was wonderful.

AMELIA. More good luck.

SCHEIN. Then we had a beautiful child. A daughter. Heather. How lucky can you get? (*pause*) Do you believe in God, Amelia?

AMELIA. No. I wish I did. It would make things easier.

SCHEIN. *I* did. Not only that. I believed that people are good. *Inherently* good. Do you believe that?

AMELIA. No, I don't.

SCHEIN. (*Adopting a professorial voice, as if recalling a college lecture class.*) "Granted, goodness can be suffocated by poverty...oppression—but it's there in our bones, in our genes." (*in his own voice*) That was my message. I taught the goodness of man. I was the eternal cockeyed optimist. My lectures—books—TV appearances—the message was always the same.

AMELIA. I guess people love to hear that.

SCHEIN. You bet they do. I was a natural for Oprah. Positive thinking. Nose to the grindstone. The religious right wasn't sure about me. I never talked about sin. But they gave me the benefit of the doubt. How do *you* feel about sin, Amelia?

AMELIA. (*thoughtfully, wading in*) If you mean, do I believe that people do terrible things—yes, I believe in sin. But if you mean they'll end up in a place called Hell—no, I don't.

SCHEIN. So there's no Heaven either?

AMELIA. (*shaking her head*) No Heaven, no Hell.

SCHEIN. (*agreeing with her*) Okay. You know, I was the darling of the liberals, too. Because I preached that we had to cure poverty and oppression.

Liberals believe you can cure anything. They just don't know how to do it. I became almost famous. I promised the City of Heaven right here on Earth! (*He raises his hands above his head.*) Halleluyah! Sounds great, doesn't it?

AMELIA. I guess so...

SCHEIN. As you said, people loved that idea. Not that it was anything new. But I backed it up with a lot of intellectual crap. That's part of the game. It's got to have *gravitas,* as we say in Academia. I was riding high. A kind of pop hero. They even gave me a nickname. You may have heard of me. I was a celebrity for a while. I was in the news. On TV.

AMELIA. I don't watch much TV.

SCHEIN. My name is Michael Schein. They called me "Professor Sunshine."

AMELIA. (*gradually realizing who he is and afraid again*) You're...? Yes, I know who you are.

SCHEIN. Amelia, relax. I'm not going to kill you. I've already killed someone—and if you do it right, once is enough. (*pause*) I sat through the trial. I listened to my friend, John—my *best* friend, John—tell the jury what he did to my daughter—to Heather. (*His voice becomes higher-pitched, weaker, as he repeats what John said.*) He said, "She was so pretty. I just wanted to touch her. That's all. But she got scared. She started to cry. She started to scream. I just wanted to stop the screaming." That's what my best friend said. And I couldn't save her.

AMELIA. (*visibly shaken, barely audible*) I'm sorry... I'm so sorry.

SCHEIN. Margery wasn't at the trial. She stopped the pain the only way she could... She *ended* it. I was all alone... Of course, he was convicted. Sentenced to life without parole.

AMELIA. *That* was something, wasn't it?

SCHEIN. My wife and my daughter were dead. And he was punished with *life?* That wasn't fair.

AMELIA. No. It wasn't.

SCHEIN. I *made* it fair. (*He lifts the revolver and looks at it as he says*) I was in the front row, a few feet behind John, when the judge read the sentence. I shot him—one—two—three times. In front of a hundred witnesses. (*He looks up at the "sky."*) "How do you like your blue-eyed boy, Mr. Death?" (*He puts the revolver down.*) I traded places with John. They sentenced *me* to life. And to be honest, it wasn't really about fairness. Or revenge.

AMELIA. Why, then?

SCHEIN. It was my fault. What happened to them.

AMELIA. No, it wasn't.

SCHEIN. It was. Too much sunshine. That can be dangerous. I was burned by it. Blinded by it.

AMELIA. You're not to blame.

SCHEIN. I am.

AMELIA. Tell me, what are you going to do now?

SCHEIN. Keep moving. For a while. What are *you* going to do?

AMELIA. Me? I don't know, but...

SCHEIN. Listen, Amelia. Take my advice. Too many dark clouds are just as bad as too much sunshine. Sell this monstrosity of a house. Get the hell out of the woods. Go to Boston and write your ass off.

AMELIA. I don't think I can do that.

SCHEIN. How come *I* can't wear you down? Everybody else does. You're not scared of me any more?

AMELIA. I'm sorry—about what happened to you.

SCHEIN. It didn't just happen. I *made* it happen. But I'm not going to spend my life in a cell. I can't.

AMELIA. They'll keep looking for you.

SCHEIN. I know they will.

AMELIA. How did you get away?

SCHEIN. That's a funny story. These two cops were driving me to the prison in Cheshire. Tough guys. One was in the back seat of the car with me. I was handcuffed. I was no problem, just a nerd who went ballistic. They were talking and laughing about a hooker they had arrested. I grabbed the guy's gun, got the keys to the handcuffs, took the car and left them cussing me on a back road. A few miles later, I hid the car in the woods. And started to run.

AMELIA. They'll be looking for you everywhere.

SCHEIN. (*standing up*) They'll find me. I'm counting on it. (*He holds up the revolver.*) The first thing I did when I left the car was empty the gun. But they don't know that.

(SCHEIN *exits.*)

AMELIA. The next morning, I listened to my sister on the local TV news. The convicted killer they called Professor Sunshine—armed and dangerous—had attacked two state troopers. They killed him. (*pause*) That afternoon I called a real estate agent. I'm selling this monstrosity of a house.

YESTERDAYS AND TOMORROWS

DANCING ON THE CEILING

CHARACTERS:
JULIA PATTERSON, *an energetic, physically active sixty-year-old woman.*
AMY BARNETT, *her daughter, a successful Manhattan attorney.*
DIANE STEINER, *Julia's seventy-year-old friend and neighbor.*

THE TIME: *An August morning before the COVID-19 pandemic.*
THE PLACE: *A leisure-community apartment in a New York City suburb.*

At intervals during the play, the music of a tango is heard softly in the background. This music re-appears occasionally, when Julia talks about the tango.

JULIA. (*softly, to herself*) I guess that does it. (*going over her mental list*) Passport: yes. Traveler's Checks: yes. Everything's packed, I hope. I *pray.* And if I *do* forget something? I can buy it *there.* We're not going to the North Pole! It's Buenos Aires! (*She sings*) "Don't cry for me, Argentina/ The truth is, I never left you…" *Marcos* has the tickets. So I don't have to worry about that. (*sighs*) But it's only nine o'clock in the morning. He won't be here for a couple of hours. And we don't take off till *four.* I guess I'll have another cup of coffee. (*She pours a cup. Drinks a sip or two.*) Waiting… I hate waiting. I've waited *much* too long. (*The doorbell rings.*) That's not Marcos. He's always late!

(*She opens the door.* DIANE STEINER *enters.*)

DIANE. Am I bothering you, Julia? Am I in the way?

JULIA. No, Diane. I've finished packing.

DIANE. Just tell me, and I'll disappear in a cloud of dust.

JULIA. I could use the company. Sit down. Have a cup of coffee.

DIANE. You're sure?

JULIA. Positive.

(*After a sip or two of coffee.*)

DIANE. So this is it, huh? The big day.

JULIA. The big day.

DIANE. I have to admit, I didn't think it would really happen.

JULIA. Me, neither. Sometimes I would say to myself, "Julia, are you crazy? You'll never go through with it."

DIANE. But you did.

JULIA. I did!

DIANE. And you're on your way!

JULIA. You know, Arthur and I…We never really traveled much. I mean, we did *go* places. To the West Coast. To Chicago. Paris once. Rome a couple of times. London.

DIANE. Sure *sounds* like a *lot* of travel.

JULIA. But it was always a *business* trip. Never a vacation. Never a time to relax. Arthur didn't know *how* to relax. And I was always on display: (*mocking the words*) the well-dressed, well-mannered wife, who makes small talk—*very* small talk—with the *other* well-dressed, well-mannered wives.

DIANE. Charlie wouldn't let *me* work. I've told you: When we got married, I was a bookkeeper at a big printing company in downtown Manhattan. Not a bad job. Charlie made me quit. He said he would be ashamed if I worked. He said people would have no respect for him. It's not like that today.

JULIA. It's a different world. My daughter and her husband are both lawyers but she's a *big* shot and he's a *little* shot. Some of her cases are *so* big, they're in the newspapers. Last year there was a story about her in the *New York Times*.

DIANE. (*musing*) A different world.

JULIA. Well, I'm going to a different world, too!

DIANE. South of the Border. *Way* south!

JULIA. I wish I was there already.

DIANE. I guess you've rehearsed everything a thousand times.

JULIA. A *million*. And I keep going over the steps in my head. Do you remember that old song, "Dancing on the Ceiling"? (*She sings*) "He dances overhead/ On the ceiling near my bed/In my sight/ Through the night."

DIANE. Oh, yeah. A real oldie.

(*Tango music begins.*)

JULIA. At night, after rehearsal days with Marcos, I lie in bed and look up at the ceiling and there we are! I go through the whole routine, over and over, dancing on the ceiling with him.

(*Music swells.*)

DIANE. Very romantic! Very sexy!

JULIA. No, no, Diane. This isn't about romance.

DIANE. Are you sure?

JULIA. Yes, I'm sure.

DIANE. (*skeptically*) I'll take your word for it.

JULIA. Marcos is a wonderful young man. But, believe me, the *only* thing we share is the tango.

(*Tango music fades out and disappears. The doorbell rings.*)

DIANE. Is that Marcos?

JULIA. No, too early. (*She opens the door.*) Amy! (*unenthusiastically*) What a surprise.

AMY. Hi, Mom. Hello, Diane.

DIANE. Hi, Amy. Nice to see you. I just dropped in for a couple of minutes.

AMY. (*unconvincingly*) You don't have to go.

DIANE. I *do*. I just wanted to say a quick *Bon Voyage*. Have a great time, Julia.

JULIA. Thank you.

DIANE. I want to hear all about it when you get back.

JULIA. You will. I promise.

(DIANE *leaves, throwing an air kiss.*)

JULIA. Would you like some coffee?

AMY. No, thanks.

JULIA. I don't think you're here for a "quick *Bon Voyage*."

AMY. Mom, you're not *really* doing this, are you?

JULIA. Of *course* I am.

AMY. I can't believe it. It's not *you*.

JULIA. You say that as if you know me. You don't.

AMY. I agree. *My* mother doesn't run off to South America to tango with a thirty-year-old gigolo.

JULIA. That's *not* what your mother is doing.

AMY. Well, what the hell *is* she doing?

JULIA. She's catching up.

AMY. Catching up with *what*?

JULIA. With all the things she didn't do for most of her life.

AMY. What are you talking about?

JULIA. I'm talking about your father.

AMY. He's probably turning over in his grave.

JULIA. I hope so.

AMY. You *hope* so?

JULIA. When your father and I got married, one of the things I admired about him was his ambition. I was sure he would be successful.

AMY. He was.

JULIA. *He* didn't think so. He was never satisfied. He kept climbing up the ladder, but there was always someone above him. Every win turned into a loss. And he never became the "top dog." The ambition I so admired in him turned sour. It became a wall between us. And then, long before he died, we just stopped loving each other. Long before *he* died, our marriage died.

AMY. I never... Why didn't I know that?

JULIA. You were too busy with your own life. He was very proud of you. So was I. So *am* I. Always at the top of your class in college. At law school. In your practice. You never let anything or anyone—including your father—stop you from doing what you wanted to do.

AMY. I admit it. *I'm* ambitious, too.

JULIA. So was your brother.

AMY. Daniel? Are you kidding?

JULIA. He just has a different *kind* of ambition.

AMY. You said it! He's living in a Greenwich Village brownstone with seven or eight other weirdos. He barely makes a living as a cartoonist. His marriage ceremony was performed by a Zen Master. And he named his son Moonbeam.

JULIA. But he's happy, Amy. He's happy. And *he* never let anything or anyone—including your father—stop him from doing what he wanted to do.

AMY. I think I'm getting the message: *you* weren't that lucky.

JULIA. It's not about luck. It's about courage. Your father was a very strong man. Overpowering. I was only twenty when I married him. A very *young* twenty. It was a time when women were starting to get their fair share. But I had no special skills. No obvious talent. No clear sense of purpose. So when your father proposed, I dropped out of college in my Junior year to get married. I was feeling trapped and just gave up on myself.

AMY. Jesus Christ, Mom!

JULIA. One good thing your father did for me: he left me a lot of money. I'm grateful for that.

AMY. So you can afford to go to Buenos Aires? With a gigolo?

JULIA. (*Shakes her head "No".*) Let me tell you a story, my dear. About a discovery I made just about a year ago. I was at a mall downtown. It was a beautiful day in late Spring and I was out leisurely window-shopping for a summer dress or two, a pair of sandals for the warm weather. (*Tango music begins softly and swells as she speaks.*) Music was literally in the air, floating out of a dance studio next to a trendy little shoe store. Music with a strong, sexy beat. I not only *heard* it, I *felt* it. It was exciting. Thrilling. *Passionate.*

AMY. God, Mother!

JULIA. I forgot about summer dresses. I forgot about *everything.* I was drawn into the studio by that music. I wanted to dance to it, *drown* in it. And that's how I met Marcos Esteban Minaya.

AMY. The gigolo?

JULIA. The dance teacher. Marcos is a very polite, proper young man. He's a professional dancer, was in the cast of a show that ran on Broadway for three years. "Tango Argentina."

AMY. I saw it. (*tongue in cheek*) I think he was the third dancer on the left.

JULIA. (*laughs*) Could be. He's *from* Buenos Aires. His family still lives there. But he fell for an American girl and stayed in the States after the show closed. She persuaded him to get out of show biz so they could have a more normal life, she said. He loved her enough to try. And he loved dancing, too. So he found a job teaching at the studio. They were still living together when I met him. She left him a couple of months ago.

(Music fades but doesn't end.)

AMY. And you've taken her place.

JULIA. No, I haven't. But I *have* learned to tango. And I'm pretty good at it. And that's what Marcos and I are going to do. In Buenos Aires! At the World Tango Championship!

AMY. Look, it's great that you love to dance, but...

(Tango music begins to build.)

JULIA. For two weeks every August, Buenos Aires *is* the Tango. Thousands of tango fans come from all over the world. There are free concerts. Classes for beginners. Workshops. And *milongas*—dance parties named for an older dance, one that came *before* the tango. And hundreds of couples, like Marcos and me, will compete to become world champions!

AMY. You don't think that *you*...

JULIA. No. Of course not. But we'll be out there, doing what's called the *Tango de Pista*. A slow dance, stylish, traditional. Just right for *me*. Think of it, Amy! Julia Patterson and Marcos Minaya performing at the World Tango Championships! The thrill of victory *(laughing)*...and the agony of defeat!

AMY. *(softly, understanding)* You really want to do this.

JULIA. I really do. And I'm sure it's not the *last* crazy thing I'm going to do.

AMY. I *hope* it's not.

JULIA. Thank you, Amy.

AMY. All I can say is—I love you, Mom.

JULIA. I love you, too, dear.

AMY. I know I won't be there to applaud for you and cheer for you, but I sure as hell *will* be rooting for you!

(*Tango music swells to a climax and ends.*)

THE DOG

CHARACTERS:
HOWARD KLEIN, *a senior citizen with an assertive point of view.*
ELLIE, *his daughter, a very successful forty-year-old lawyer.*

THE TIME: *The present.*
THE PLACE: *The family room of a home in a New York City suburb.*

As the action begins, HOWARD and ELLIE are seated in comfortable chairs, a coffee table between them. An open wine bottle is on the table. They are drinking wine.

HOWARD. You know, Ellie, this is one of my favorite times. After dinner, sharing a bottle of Cabernet in the family room with my daughter. Catching up.

ELLIE. (*without much conviction*) I guess it's been too long.

HOWARD. It has. (*overlooking the insincerity, more upbeat*) So tell me, is my famous beef stew as delicious as ever?

ELLIE. (*with more conviction*) You bet it is. It's a taste *thrill*. I don't know how you do it. I think you could have been a master chef.

HOWARD. And I wasted all those years as a lawyer.

ELLIE. It's never too late to shift gears!

HOWARD. I think my gears have just about had it. Another shift and I'll end up in Reverse!

ELLIE. Well, at least you made one *small* change: you finally took my advice and got a dog.

HOWARD. *Your* advice—and just about everyone *else's*. All the "experts." (*pompously, satirically, as if quoting the experts*) "Senior citizens who live alone are much happier when they share their lives with a dog. And walking a dog is *marvelous* exercise."

ELLIE. That's true.

HOWARD. (*continuing as an expert*) "You have someone to talk to." (*parenthetically, in his own voice*) And it's someone who can't talk *back*. (*in the expert's voice again*) "And *feeding* a dog may remind your decaying brain that *you* haven't eaten lately."

ELLIE. Well, you're making fun of me, but we always had a dog, didn't we?

HOWARD. Yes. Golden Labs, all of them.

ELLIE. I remember Amadeus. And Buster. And Cookie.

HOWARD. You know, you were away at school, at Georgetown, when Cookie went to that great cookie jar in the sky, and we just didn't have the heart—or the *energy*—to replace him.

ELLIE. Mom loved pampering the dogs.

HOWARD. She loved pampering *all* of us.

ELLIE. I know how much you miss her.

HOWARD. This isn't how it's supposed to be. The rule is: *Husbands* die first. It's been almost three years and I still miss her every day, every night.

ELLIE. Of course you do. That's why you have to keep active. *That's* why I thought you should get a dog.

HOWARD. Dog or no dog, I'm *plenty* active. I'm at the Senior Center two, three times a week. See a movie sometimes. Have lunch. Play pool.

ELLIE. Hah! And deprive those poor bastards of their Social Security checks.

HOWARD. No, no, that's not how it is. We just bet a *couple* of dollars a game, Ellie. They don't mind. They *know* I'm a shark. It gives them something to live for: to beat me at my own game.

ELLIE. And then you go home to an empty house and brood.

HOWARD. I *never* brood. I watch TV. I read. It's like there's a big sign over the fireplace: "No brooding allowed."

ELLIE. Well, you haven't convinced me.

HOWARD. It might help if I saw my daughter more often. Not to mention my grandchildren.

ELLIE. I know. We haven't been here—as a family—for...

HOWARD. Look, I know why Stan and I never really clicked.

ELLIE. He's just so busy that...

HOWARD. (*interrupting her*) We come from different worlds. His parents have money. He's got a J.D. from Harvard Law School. I had to *work* my way through Brooklyn Law. And I never had a big-time practice like the two of you.

ELLIE. That doesn't matter.

HOWARD. It matters to *him*. I understand that. But I miss the *kids*. How are they doing? What are they up to?

ELLIE. Gregory's playing soccer now. He loves it. And Laurie is writing poems. Can you believe that?

HOWARD. Sure I can. Your Mom used to write poetry. Don't you remember? Some of her poems were published.

ELLIE. Yes, I remember. But you can't make a *living* doing that.

HOWARD. Maybe not. But poetry isn't just a talent. It's a different way of looking at things. Your Mom had that gift. Maybe Laurie does, too.

ELLIE. Maybe. I'll bring them for a visit soon. I promise.

HOWARD. That'd be great.

ELLIE. (*changing the mood*) So tell me about your dog. Where is he, by the way?

HOWARD. He's upstairs in my bedroom. He doesn't like strangers.

ELLIE. I hope I can win him over.

HOWARD. Don't count on it.

ELLIE. I guess he's no pushover.

HOWARD. That's putting it mildly. He's a rescue dog from a shelter. He cost me twenty-five bucks and they were glad to get rid of him.

ELLIE. What's wrong with him?

HOWARD. He looks awful. He's a mutt, with a trace of Golden Lab in him. He's about a year old, maybe a little more, and he must have been through hell. One of his ears is half chewed up and he has a couple of scars on his belly.

ELLIE. So why did you buy him?

HOWARD. Well, this is going to sound a little weird, but he was...*dignified.* He didn't try to charm me when I passed his cage. He didn't bark or beg. He just sat there and looked me in the eye, as if to say, "What you see is what you get." I liked that. He reminded me...of *me.*

ELLIE. Who could ask for anything more?

HOWARD. We get along fine.

ELLIE. Of course you do.

HOWARD. He never barks. He's so well behaved they let me bring him to the Senior Center, which is strictly against the rules. He follows me around quietly, watches me play pool, takes a couple of scraps from me when I eat lunch there and never bothers anybody.

ELLIE. You should teach *him* to play pool. The two of you could make a fortune!

HOWARD. (*going along with the joke*) That's a hell of a good idea!

ELLIE. And walking him *is* good exercise, isn't it?

HOWARD. Yes, it is. We often go to the Cascades. Where Mom and I used to walk with you and Andrew—when you were kids.

ELLIE. I remember. That's a beautiful place. All those winding, shady trails through the woods.

HOWARD. And the little waterfall. Not exactly Niagara...

ELLIE. *Better* than Niagara. You could reach out and feel the ice-cold water running through your fingers.

HOWARD. When we lived in the city, before you were born, Mom and I loved strolling the parks there, too—the crown jewel, Central Park, and quieter Riverside Park. But I'll never forget when she said that city *trees* were like city *people*: they've lost their innocence. Small-town trees—like the ones in the Cascades—*haven't* lost it. That's the way she saw things—the way poets see things.

ELLIE. She didn't pass that along to me, that way of seeing things.

HOWARD. It may have skipped a generation—and found your daughter.

ELLIE. Maybe so.

HOWARD. We've got some friends in the Cascades—the dog and I. There's a skinny old guy named Sylvester who has two frisky Dalmatians—Hope and Charity. They dance around my dog and he'll watch them, maybe run a few steps with them. But he mostly keeps to himself. They seem to respect him.

ELLIE. *Respect* him?

HOWARD. That's right. So does Sylvester. He once said, "Your dog is a *gentleman*. You know what I mean?"

ELLIE. A pool shark and a gentleman. Quite a combination!

HOWARD. We have another friend: Amanda, a real high-pressure character. Young, nervous. Never stops talking. Her dog—Fifi—is a lazy Collie. No gumption. No spirit. "Sometimes she sits down and won't move at all," Amanda says. "I have to *carry* her to the car!"

ELLIE. Lots of drama in the Cascades, huh?

HOWARD. I guess there is. And there are memories, too, lots of memories. Of Mom. And you and Andrew, when you were kids.

ELLIE. You know, Dad, you keep saying, "the dog." What's his name?

HOWARD. He doesn't *have* a name.

ELLIE. He doesn't? Why not?

HOWARD. (*seeming not to hear her question*) The walk at the Cascades is good exercise. But if the weather is bad, or I'm just not in the mood, I let the dog out loose in the back yard for a while. There's no fence around the yard, but I know he won't run away. He's been out in the world. He knows how hard life can be out there and he's never going back to it.

ELLIE. So I guess I was right about you getting a dog, wasn't I?

HOWARD. We get along well. He doesn't ask for much. Two meals a day. A good walk. I can even let him go out on his own and he won't run away.

ELLIE. And you have someone to...love.

HOWARD. (*emphatically, almost harshly*) No. He doesn't ask for *my* love. And I don't ask for *his*. We understand each other.

ELLIE. Well, okay. But at least give him a *name*.

HOWARD. Your brother Andrew had a name, and we lost him when he was only six. Your mother had a name. And I lost *her*. You have a name and I've lost you, too.

ELLIE. No, Dad, you didn't lose me. I still...

HOWARD. (*interrupting her*) My dog doesn't need a name. I give him what *he* needs. He gives me what *I* need. He doesn't mind being "the dog." It works for us.

ELLIE. (*softly*) I guess it *does* work for you. *Both* of you.

À LA RECHERCHE
DU TEMPS PERDU

CHARACTERS:
EDWARD HUNTER, *a fiftyish American, well-to-do, well-dressed, well-groomed.*
SIMONE ARNAUD, *a fiftyish French woman, stylishly-dressed, stylishly-groomed.*

THE TIME: *A September afternoon, a few years ago.*
THE PLACE: *A sidewalk cafe on the Boulevard Saint Germain in Paris.*

As the action begins, EDWARD *enters, sees* SIMONE *seated at a table and approaches her.*

EDWARD. (*hesitantly, his French words poorly pronounced*) Excuse me... uh... *Excusez-moi, Madame.*

SIMONE. (*reading a newspaper, looks up, annoyed*) Are you lost, *Monsieur?* The Seine is *that* way. The *Jardin du Luxembourg...(very slowly, as if she is talking to a child)* the...Luxembourg...Garden...is *that* way. And Times Square is a bit further.

(*She goes back to reading the newspaper.*)

EDWARD. I didn't mean to disturb you...

SIMONE. And yet you have succeeded.

EDWARD. (*still tentative*) I thought—I *think* I recognize you.

SIMONE. I doubt that very much.

EDWARD. I may be wrong. It's been a long, long time.

SIMONE. (*slyly*) A hundred years ago, *peut-être*?

EDWARD. Not quite that long. Are you...Simone Arnaud?

SIMONE. (*surprised*) *Oui*, that was my...(*struggling to find the English words*)...my "maiden" name. (*angrily*) How would you know that?

EDWARD. I'm Edward Hunter, Simone. Remember? I was your "sexy Eddie." Though it was ages ago.

SIMONE. (*scrutinizing him*) Hmmm... You are very...different. But, yes, I begin to see a hint of you. Just a hint. (*sighs*) Time changes everything, *n'est-ce pas*?

EDWARD. Maybe not. I don't remember the fancy French expression for it, but "The more things change, the more they remain the same." Isn't that so?

SIMONE. *Mais non*. I don't believe it. It sounds like wisdom, but it is not so.

EDWARD. May I join you? Please. For old time's sake?

SIMONE. If you must. It was so long ago. A different world. A different Simone.

(*He sits at the table.*)

EDWARD. Not to me. (*a bit too poetically to be sincere*) You're as beautiful now as you were that September morning, when we first met.

SIMONE. (*pleased despite her reservations*) My mirror, when I look in it each day—that is not what I see.

EDWARD. That is what *I* see, Simone. What a wonderful Autumn that was! The best Autumn of my life. Unforgettable.

SIMONE. You were so young... Eddie.

EDWARD. Twenty-two. It was right after a summer at my parents' lake house. I had just graduated from college.

SIMONE. Always, I remember you would say "Harvard" the way an *artiste* says "Picasso" or a *chanteuse* says "Piaf."

EDWARD. Yes, Harvard. It was important to me then. Hey, I was just a kid.

SIMONE. I was also young. But not so much a "kid" as you.

EDWARD. No, not at all. You were much more *grown up*.

SIMONE. *Oui*, very much more.

EDWARD. After that summer at the lake, my father gave me my graduation present: a month in Paris.

SIMONE. A very nice *Papa*, yes?

EDWARD. Yes. And a few days after I arrived, I saw you at that little bistro—I forget the name of it...

SIMONE. *Bien sûr*. I too have forgotten.

EDWARD. I said to myself, "There's the girl of my dreams."

SIMONE. Did you dream *en Français*? *Très charmant*.

EDWARD. Hah! You should know better than anyone: after two years of French classes, I *couldn't* dream in French. I could hardly *say* or *understand* anything.

SIMONE. But always you were so proud about that.

EDWARD. Was I?

SIMONE. As if to be ignorant is a good thing.

EDWARD. Of course, it's *not* a good thing. *(trying to regain the upper hand)* But I didn't have to know your language to fall in love with you.

SIMONE. *(smiling, remembering)* Ahhh... I am drinking with my friends—Henri and Juliette—and Albert, too. And here comes this American boy who tells us—in English—he will buy us a bottle of the best wine—*if* he can drink it with us.

EDWARD. Yes, that's what I said!

SIMONE. I'm the only one who speaks a little English, and I tell you to come and share the wine with us.

EDWARD. So you *do* remember?

SIMONE. *(softly, regretfully)* *Oui*, I remember.

EDWARD. And afterwards I invited you to my apartment...

SIMONE. *(remembering with pleasure)* For us—we were poor students—it was *(with exaggerated awe)* *un grand appartement élégant*. On the *Quai aux Fleurs*...

EDWARD. You could look down at the river...

SIMONE. And across at *la Rive Droit*.

EDWARD. You stayed with me that night—and almost every night after that. At the end of September, I asked my father for another month—and he gave it to me. To us.

SIMONE. It is a good thing to have a rich *Papa*.

EDWARD. I never regretted it. We had fun, didn't we? You and I—with your friends, too, sometimes. Wandering all over the city. You took me everywhere, showed me everything. We ate too much, drank too much, went to the theater—where I could only guess what they were saying—but I didn't care.

SIMONE. And the ballet—no words to worry about. And the *opéra,* too: but who cares what they are saying? They love, they sing and—*souvent*—they die.

EDWARD. (*moving to safer ground*) We went to parties and we made our *own* parties, too.

SIMONE. You were a very good dancer. That, I remember. I called you my Nijinsky, didn't I?

EDWARD. You did, and 'til you explained it, I thought it was a French curse! Or maybe a Russian one!

SIMONE. Ha! You were never... (*reaching for the word*) "shy." You play the guitar all the time and sing. Not very good, I regret to say.

EDWARD. Badly. I admit it. Everyone cheered when I junked the guitar.

SIMONE. And when you are back in the States, did you do what you say you would?

EDWARD. And what was that?

SIMONE. You would say to your *Papa,* "No, I will not come and work with you! I will be a *journaliste.*"

EDWARD. He wanted me to be a broker like him. Work on Wall Street. Make a lot of money.

SIMONE. Your nice rich *Papa,* yes?

EDWARD. Yes. But I told him I wanted to be a reporter. You see, I knew this guy at school...

SIMONE. (*with exaggerated awe*) At *Har-vard?*

EDWARD. (*a little embarrassed*) Yes. And when he talked about the life reporters lead—covering the big stories—the most important people... It really sounded exciting. It sounded like the job I wanted.

SIMONE. Did you do this? Become a *journaliste?*

EDWARD. (*evading a direct answer*) My father wasn't happy about it, but he had a client who owned a big-city newspaper. He said he'd call him. He'd made money for the guy so he owed my Dad. I told him I didn't want his help. I wanted to make it on my own.

SIMONE. Bravo, Eddie! Bravo!

EDWARD. So I started at the bottom of the ladder. On my own.

SIMONE. Was it so exciting, that job?

EDWARD. Big mistake. I was just a glorified copy boy. Never saw any real action. It was a complete dead end. I stuck with it for about a year.

SIMONE. You don't like "the bottom," Eddie. You were never there before. So what did you do? You ask your *Papa* to help?

EDWARD. No...I...gave up that idea and just settled into a job at his firm.

SIMONE. Ah! And you do very well, too? Just like him.

EDWARD. (*with no pride*) Yes. Just like him. It's amazing what you can do with other people's money.

SIMONE. You are married?

EDWARD. Yes. We were very happy for...years. But it doesn't seem the same any more.

SIMONE. You have a family? Children?

EDWARD. We have a son, Jack. He's a jazz drummer, very talented. Has lots of fans, including us, and we're proud of him. But he lives in Chicago and he tours a lot—so we don't see him very often. Our daughter, Sarah, is very close to her mother. She married a professor at Columbia...who's old enough to be her father. He's a bit of a stuffed shirt. (*without pleasure*) We see them a little *too* often.

SIMONE. You are not happy, Eddie, and this is why you come to Paris?

EDWARD. Yes. That's why I'm here.

SIMONE. You have not come back before?

EDWARD. I have. But never alone, the way it was the first time.

SIMONE. And what did you think you would find?

EDWARD. (*with feigned innocence*) I don't know... I'm not sure.

SIMONE. Did you think you would be walking on the *Boulevard Saint Germain* and, by chance, see me here? (*with a hint of suspicion*) Or *was* it by chance?

EDWARD. Actually...it wasn't—it *isn't* by chance.

SIMONE. Ah, so you are not sexy young Eddie now. You are (*with mock deference*) Mr. Edward Hunter.

EDWARD. I...did some research.

SIMONE. So you know all about me?

EDWARD. I know you're a fashion designer, a successful one, and Paris Fashion Week will be here in a few days. Your husband Michel is—(*with ironic emphasis*) a journalist. And your daughter Marguerite is a writer, too. A novelist. And you often have lunch here, alone, even when you're very busy.

SIMONE. You know many things about me, Eddie. Do you know also that I am very happy? So again I ask, why are you here?

EDWARD. I don't know—I just wanted to connect with my past—with a time when *I* was happy, too.

SIMONE. (*kindly*) Eddie, life is not a *roman*, a novel. In a novel, you take a bite of a *madeleine*—a little cake—and see the whole past clearly, perfectly. But *only* in a novel. Your happy time here was not the way you remember it.

EDWARD. Well, I may have forgotten some things, but...

SIMONE. (*interrupting*) Do you know why we wanted to be with you? It was not your dancing, no, or—*mon Dieu*!--your singing. Or your handsome face. It was your *money*. We were poor students, Eddie. But with you, we could go to the theater, ballet, *opéra*, have the best seats. Drink the best wine. Eat the best food. And live in *un appartement élégant*.

EDWARD. I know that. But you and I had something special, didn't we?

SIMONE. Did we?

EDWARD. Remember when we drove down to Angers to see your Uncle? We stopped on the way at this charming little hotel and I asked for the most expensive room.

SIMONE. *Oui*. And they said we could have the Bridal Suite.

EDWARD. And when we went down to the dining room, you wanted the cozy little table for two that was by the window, looking out at the woods. And the *mâitre d'* said, "But, of course: it is reserved for the Bridal Suite." So we got it!

SIMONE. He even gave us *une demi-bouteille de Champagne*.

EDWARD. To celebrate our (*said with attempt at French pronunciation*) "*mariage!*" That was special, wasn't it?

SIMONE. (*reluctantly*) I suppose, yes.

EDWARD. (*following up his lead*) And that night in October, at dinner, when we met the Director of the *Orsay* Museum, and you talked him into giving us a sneak preview of a show.

SIMONE. *Oui*, it was—the *ouevre*—the paintings of Mary Cassatt.

EDWARD. Just the two of us in the empty *Orsay*, late at night. That was special—that was magic wasn't it?

SIMONE. It was. A little magic, *oui*.

EDWARD. So we *did* have something special, didn't we?

SIMONE. *Non*, Eddie, not in the way you mean it. When you knew me, I loved Henri. It was Henri *before* you—and *after* you. And now and then, *while* I was with you—until we finished *université* and we all went our separate ways.

EDWARD. Henri? So "sexy Eddie" was all a lie.

SIMONE. (*gently*) Not *all* of it. You were *naïf*—so "innocent." We *did* have something together. But not what you believe it was.

EDWARD. I don't know what to say.

SIMONE. Eddie, if the past you remember is true or not true, it does not matter. We cannot go back there. We have only today and tomorrow.

EDWARD. The way things are, I'm not sure I even have *that* now.

SIMONE. And why not? You say you were happy with your wife for years. And now it is not the same.

EDWARD. It doesn't *feel* the same—the way it used to be.

SIMONE. *Bien sûr.* You are different people now than when you were young. But does that mean your love has died?

EDWARD. (*thoughtfully*) I... I don't know.

SIMONE. *Mariage* is not easy. For anyone. We, too, *mon mari*—my husband and I—not so long ago, we have a difficult time—*très difficile.*

EDWARD. What did you do?

SIMONE. One night, we talked...and talked...and talked. All night, into the morning. Telling truth to each other. Remembering why we are together.

EDWARD. And you stayed together.

SIMONE. Yes, we are *still* together. Still *happy* together.

EDWARD. I wonder...

SIMONE. And your children? Do you try to be closer to them? Do you tell your son you want to see him more?

EDWARD. Well, we don't want to *force* him to come.

SIMONE. Does he know you are proud of him?

EDWARD. He *must* know that!

SIMONE. *Mon Dieu!* You must tell him, Eddie! Tell him you are proud of him! And tell him you want to see him!

EDWARD. Yes, I could... I should...

SIMONE. Your daughter. You do not like her *mari*? He is a bad person?

EDWARD. No, no. And he's been good to her. It's just—he's almost as old as I am!

SIMONE. Old enough to be her father?

EDWARD. Yes, old enough.

SIMONE. Then *peut-être* she misses her father—she is looking for a father. But *you* are her *Papa*, yes?

EDWARD. I am.

SIMONE. Then *be* her *Papa*!

EDWARD. I never thought of it that way.

SIMONE. And her husband. Can you forgive him?

EDWARD. (*sheepishly*) Well... I guess so. They do seem happy together.

SIMONE. There is a saying: *Autres temps, autres moeurs*. It means "in other times, people do things in different ways." Eddie, the other times—the old times—do not matter now. You must find different ways for *today*—and *tomorrow*—to make you happy. I cannot do this for you. You must do it for yourself.

EDWARD. (*smiles sadly*) I know you're right.

SIMONE. Do not look back, Eddie. Look forward.

EDWARD. I'll try, Simone. I'll try. You've given me a lot to think about. I don't know how it'll all work out, but I *will* try.

SIMONE. So maybe, after all, you find what you are looking for in Paris?

EDWARD. Maybe so. (*after a beat*) May I ask you for a favor?

SIMONE. A favor?

EDWARD. Would you have a glass of wine with me before I go? Let's say for old time's sake—even if those old times never were.

SIMONE. *Mais non*, Eddie. We will toast to your *future*—and the *new* times—the new ways you will find happiness.

EDWARD. My future?

SIMONE. *Oui*, your future.

EDWARD. *D'accord*, I'll drink to that!

MARY ANNE

CHARACTERS:
THE WIFE, *a soft-spoken, patient woman in her seventies.*
THE HUSBAND, *a man in his seventies, whose memory is failing.*

THE TIME: *An April morning.*
THE PLACE: *The porch of a lakeside summer home in Connecticut.*

As the action begins, the HUSBAND *enters.*

WIFE. (*seated at the table, drinking coffee*) Good morning, dear.

HUSBAND. (*unsmiling*) Morning. (*pause*) Another morning.

(*He looks around aimlessly for a moment, sits down at the table.*)

WIFE. It's a beautiful day, isn't it? Look at the sun shining on the lake.

HUSBAND. It's too bright. Too bright. Hurts my eyes.

WIFE. The sky is clear. There's not a cloud anywhere.

HUSBAND. Tell me: What month is it?

WIFE. It's April, dear.

HUSBAND. (*under his breath, tentatively*) April showers... April showers...

WIFE. (*encouraging the memory*) Bring May flowers. That's right, dear. That's right.

HUSBAND. Can't have showers—without clouds. (*He laughs, a short, sharp laugh.*) No clouds. Guess it isn't April.

WIFE. Oh, it's just a gift from Mother Nature: a cloudless April day. (*After a couple of beats*) Would you like some breakfast, dear?

HUSBAND. (*vaguely, unfocused*) Ummmm... Breakfast...

WIFE. Coffee? (*She pours him a cup.*) I could scramble some eggs. Fry up some bacon.

HUSBAND. I don't like eggs. Hate eggs. Always did.

WIFE. You *used* to enjoy scrambled eggs. The way I whipped them up and made them light and sunny.

HUSBAND. I hate eggs!

WIFE. All right, dear. What would you like instead.

HUSBAND. (*considering the possibilities*) I want...something sweet. A muffin. Toasted. With jelly. Yes, a muffin. Jelly. Grape jelly.

WIFE. I'll make it for you. Won't take but a moment. Be right back.

HUSBAND. That's what I want.

(HUSBAND *drinks coffee. He picks up the newspaper, riffles through the pages, stops and reads an item. He looks up from the paper, puzzled, squints as if he's trying to remember something, throws the paper down on the table.*)

WIFE. (*offstage voice*) Coming, just one more minute.

HUSBAND. (*under his breath.*) April showers... May flowers. Showers. Flowers. (*loudly*) Goddammit!

WIFE. (*still offstage*) What did you say, dear?

HUSBAND. Nothing.

WIFE. (*Re-enters. She puts the plate in front of him.*) Here's something sweet for you.

HUSBAND. (*staring down at the plate*) Something sweet. (*He takes a bite of the muffin, drinks some coffee.*) Molly is sweet, isn't she?

WIFE. Yes, dear, she is.

HUSBAND. She's our daughter. A sweet girl.

WIFE. Very sweet. (*after a beat*) But a grown woman now.

HUSBAND. (*puzzled*) She's a young girl, isn't she?

WIFE. (*cautiously*) That's the way you—the way *we*—remember her, of course. But she's forty years old now. Has children of her own. Michael and Jennifer. Our grandchildren.

HUSBAND. I don't like the boys she goes out with.

WIFE. You never did.

HUSBAND. She's too good for them.

WIFE. It seemed that way, didn't it?

HUSBAND. She gets mad when I tell her. (*laughs*) Boy, does she get mad!

WIFE. That's Molly all right. Sweet and mad.

HUSBAND. One of these days, she's going to get married.

WIFE. (*patiently*) She *is* married, dear.

HUSBAND. So young and married already?

WIFE. She's not a little girl any more.

HUSBAND. (*echoing sadly*) Not a little girl any more.

WIFE. She married Robert. She met him when they were going to college. UConn.

HUSBAND. (*puzzled*) Yukon? Alaska?

WIFE. (*patiently*) The University of Connecticut. A very good school.

HUSBAND. (*reaching for the memory*) Robert. Tall, thin. A teacher, right?

WIFE. That's right, dear. They live in Ridgefield.

HUSBAND. That's not far from here, is it?

WIFE. Just a half hour away. We were there for a very nice lunch two Sundays ago. You *loved* the chocolate cake.

HUSBAND. What did I think of Robert?

WIFE. You liked him. He may be the *only* one you ever liked.

HUSBAND. (*smiles*) But she married him anyway.

WIFE. (*nodding, pleased with his humor*) That *is* funny!

HUSBAND. Are they happy?

WIFE. Yes, they're happy.

HUSBAND. I wonder...

WIFE. What do you wonder?

HUSBAND. There must be happy marriages.

WIFE. Of course there are. Lots of people have...

HUSBAND. (*interrupting, impatiently*) Most marriages are unhappy.

WIFE. Why do you say that?

HUSBAND. Because it's true.

WIFE. Ohhh, I don't think so.

HUSBAND. (*thinks for a moment*) Our son. David. An unhappy marriage. A very unhappy marriage. (*pause*) He never did anything right.

WIFE. (*softly*) Of course he did. He was a good student, very smart. Lots of Honors classes. *Always* one of the best.

HUSBAND. I don't remember that.

WIFE. We were so proud of him.

HUSBAND. Does he live in Ridgefield?

WIFE. No. He went out to California.

HUSBAND. Too far to drive.

WIFE. Much too far.

HUSBAND. Why did he go so far away?

WIFE. After the divorce, he lost his job, his confidence. He felt aimless. He went out West, hoping to make a fresh start.

HUSBAND. Why were we so proud of him?

WIFE. Ohh, when he was a student, and then those early years when he was first starting out... He had such a bright future... That's when we were proud of him.

HUSBAND. Not any more.

WIFE. But we still love him.

HUSBAND. We still love him? Why?

WIFE. You don't stop loving someone, just because they're having... problems.

HUSBAND. When *do* you stop loving them?

WIFE. You don't stop. You never stop. You *shouldn't* stop.

HUSBAND. Even if you're not proud of them any more?

WIFE. *Especially* if you're not.

HUSBAND. Wouldn't that be the best time to stop?

WIFE. But that's when they need you the most.

HUSBAND. What can I do for David? I can't do anything for him.

WIFE. We've been able to help him.

HUSBAND. Did we find him a job?

WIFE. We've loaned him some money to help him move on.

HUSBAND. When is he paying us back?

WIFE. When he can.

HUSBAND. (*after a long beat*) I dream sometimes. I dream.

WIFE. What do you dream about?

HUSBAND. I'm walking down the street. People say "hello" to me. People I know. They say "hello" to me. I go into a big building. They know me. "Hello." "How are you today?" "How's the family?"

WIFE. Is it your office building? Where you used to work?

HUSBAND. (*unsure*) My office building...

WIFE. Do you go to your office?

HUSBAND. (*grasps at the idea*) Ye-e-e-s... I go to my office. Sit down at my desk. There are folders and papers on my desk. I look at them.

WIFE. You're back at work.

HUSBAND. (*losing his confidence*) I can't read the papers. They're all blurry. (*with increasing anxiety*) I can't read them. Don't know where I am. Why I'm there. What I'm supposed to be doing. Don't know.

WIFE. It's only a dream, dear.

HUSBAND. (*frightened*) Don't know. Even when I wake up.

WIFE. (*softly*) I wish I could make it better for you.

HUSBAND. (*after a beat*) How long have we been married?

WIFE. Forty-four years. Forty-five in June.

HUSBAND. We wanted to be happy.

WIFE. We *were* happy.

HUSBAND. I don't remember being happy.

WIFE. (*sweetly*) We were, dear, most of the time, weren't we?

HUSBAND. I don't remember.

WIFE. Our first home—an apartment—was in Stamford. A third floor walk-up. We had an electric stove and I left a pot on the burner too long. (*laughs*) I almost burned a hole in the kitchen ceiling.

HUSBAND. (*unable to remember*) Stamford?

WIFE. We didn't have much, but we were happy there.

HUSBAND. When did we stop being happy?

WIFE. We didn't stop.

HUSBAND. Are you happy now?

WIFE. Yes, I am.

HUSBAND. I'm not.

WIFE. That's because of your...problems.

HUSBAND. I think of our lives—sometimes I can remember— sometimes. Not everything. Some things.

WIFE. What do you remember?

HUSBAND. I don't remember being happy.

WIFE. (*softly*) We were... We really were.

HUSBAND. Molly did things—we didn't want her to do. Didn't she?

WIFE. Yes. There was a time—drugs, the wrong kind of people.

HUSBAND. Sweet little Molly.

WIFE. That wasn't a good time.

HUSBAND. We weren't happy. Did David make us happy?

WIFE. Yes, he did.

HUSBAND. Not any more.

WIFE. He's still a young man. I have hope.

HUSBAND. (*After a long beat*) I should have gone to law school.

WIFE. I told you to go.

HUSBAND. You didn't mean it.

WIFE. I *did* mean it. I did.

HUSBAND. You *said* it but you didn't *mean* it.

WIFE. That was so long ago. A million years ago.

HUSBAND. I knew you didn't mean it. You were pregnant. I had to start making money.

WIFE. We would have found a way.

HUSBAND. Law school. That was what I wanted. I never went.

WIFE. I really am sorry.

HUSBAND. I started the grind. The grind.

WIFE. You did very well.

HUSBAND. (*pause*) Bees. Buzzing. A bee hive.

WIFE. Is this another dream?

HUSBAND. Workers. Drones. Buzzing.

WIFE. I don't know what you mean, dear.

HUSBAND. Building little wax boxes. Millions of boxes. Over and over. Nameless. Faceless. Drones. Sitting in my office, I could hear the buzzing.

WIFE. You took good care of your family, dear.

HUSBAND. I told David once—I remember—he was in high school, I think—I told him not to give up his dreams. "Don't give up your dreams!" He said, "I don't have any dreams. I don't know what I want to do with my life."

WIFE. He said that?

HUSBAND. Yes. I remember. I remember. He had no dreams. Why not?

WIFE. I don't know.

HUSBAND. Was that our fault?

WIFE. I don't think so.

HUSBAND. I hope not.

WIFE. (*After a long silence*) The first summer we came here, when Molly was just a year old... Oh, that was a wonderful summer!

HUSBAND. (*exhausted; softly*) Tell me. Tell me...

WIFE. We rented a tiny cabin for a week. It was on the other side of the lake. One room. A kitchenette. It even had indoor plumbing. And a double bed. We brought a portable crib that converted into a playpen.

HUSBAND. David was a baby?

WIFE. David wasn't born yet. Molly was a year old.

HUSBAND. Sweet Molly. Sweet Molly.

WIFE. (*happily*) We had picnics in the woods. You took us out on the lake in a rowboat... You rowed very well, dear... And we hiked all over the place. Even did some fishing.

HUSBAND. Did we catch anything?

WIFE. Nothing big enough to eat. But it was fun.

HUSBAND. We spent the summer here?

WIFE. No. We couldn't afford that. Just a week.

HUSBAND. Were we happy?

WIFE. Yes, dear, we were.

HUSBAND. I don't remember that.

WIFE. I wish you could. There were the family parties, too. Your mother and father would come. And mine. Your brother Joe and his wife, and their kids. My sister Anne. Thanksgiving. Christmas. Everyone would bring a favorite dish. Or a pie. So much noise. So much laughter.

HUSBAND. My brother?

WIFE. Joe. His wife Sharon.

HUSBAND. (*trying to remember*) Joe... Sharon...

WIFE. He died ten—no, must be twelve years ago. She passed away just two years later.

HUSBAND. Passed away... My parents passed away?

WIFE. Yes, dear. Long ago.

HUSBAND. "Passed away" sounds nicer than "died."

WIFE. I guess that's why people say it.

HUSBAND. It isn't nicer because you call it something else. (*pause*) I'm going to be dead soon.

WIFE. Don't say that.

HUSBAND. Why not?

WIFE. You can live a long time.

HUSBAND. Do you think I want to?

WIFE. I don't want to lose you.

HUSBAND. Lose me?

WIFE. I love you.

HUSBAND. You've already lost me.

WIFE. I haven't!

HUSBAND. Little pieces of me are left. Fewer every day. I've lost myself.

WIFE. You're still the man I married.

HUSBAND. Not for long.

WIFE. Please don't say that.

HUSBAND. I'm *not* scared to die. But I'm afraid to disappear.

WIFE. I'll be here. I'll be with you.

HUSBAND. I'm losing touch... With everything.

WIFE. Don't say that!

HUSBAND. You'll be a stranger. Everyone will be.

WIFE. (*beginning to cry*) Please, don't say that.

HUSBAND. I'll be a stranger. I won't know me.

WIFE. You still remember some things.

HUSBAND. Bad things. The good things are disappearing. Like me.

WIFE. I'll help you remember.

HUSBAND. We were proud of David? Good student?

WIFE. That's right.

HUSBAND. I remember his failures. His divorce. Jobs he lost. Nothing else. Not success... Not pride.

WIFE. We were proud...

HUSBAND. You talk about Molly's husband. Children. I remember her taking drugs. Fighting drugs. Losing... That's all I remember.

WIFE. But she *won*. Finally, she *won*.

HUSBAND. Soon, thank God, I won't remember bad things. But who will I be? Who will I be?

WIFE. My husband. My love.

HUSBAND. Without memories?

WIFE. Don't leave me. Please don't leave me.

HUSBAND. It's not up to me.

WIFE. I wish I could do something. I wish, I wish...

HUSBAND. Some memories—old memories—still there.

WIFE. From your childhood? Tell me.

HUSBAND. I'm tired. I'm so tired. I want to sleep.

WIFE. Tell me your memories.

HUSBAND. Growing up...with that girl next door. A little younger than me.

WIFE. You remember her?

HUSBAND. I do.

WIFE. Do you remember her name?

HUSBAND. Mary Anne.

WIFE. Tell me about Mary Anne.

HUSBAND. Very pretty.

WIFE. A pretty little lady?

HUSBAND. No. A "tom-boy." She liked sports and was as good as us boys.

WIFE. A pretty little tom-boy.

HUSBAND. We did lots of things together, had fun together... Best friends.

WIFE. Mmmm... That sounds like a love affair in the making.

HUSBAND. (*yawning*) So tired. I want to sleep.

WIFE. Oh, not just yet. Tell me more. About Mary Anne.

HUSBAND. Good friends... Best friends... All those years.

WIFE. And you can remember her now?

HUSBAND. (*getting sleepier, answering as if in a dream*) I wonder... I wonder what my life would've been if I'd married her. Would it all have been different? Better?

WIFE. What do you think, dear?

HUSBAND. It was simple then. We were going to win. We *knew* that we would win.

WIFE. That's what we thought.

HUSBAND. (*sleepier*) Why do I remember that? The one good thing I remember.

WIFE. I don't know why, dear... But it's a beautiful thing to remember.

HUSBAND. Mary Anne. Pretty. Wonderful smile. I remember.

WIFE. I'm glad you do.

HUSBAND. (*beginning to fall asleep*) Soon I won't remember. (*yawns*) What if I had married Mary Anne?

(*He falls asleep.*)

WIFE. (*a long beat*) My poor lost boy. I am Mary Anne.

THE PARTS WE PLAY

HOME BODIES

CHARACTERS:
NATHAN, *a man in his seventies, who always speaks with authority.*
MAGGIE, *a woman in her thirties, impatient, volatile.*
ELEANOR, *a still pretty, weary fifty-year-old woman.*
DANIEL, *her husband, a man in his fifties, with a good-natured, not-too-intelligent manner.*
ADAM, *a man in his twenties, soft-spoken, self-confident.*
JONATHAN, *a man in his thirties, snobbish but insecure.*

THE TIME: *The month of May.*
THE PLACE: *The living room-dining room of a cramped, dingy, unattractive house in northwestern Connecticut. The furnishings, pictures and decorations display a hodge-podge of styles, like random purchases from garage sales. There is an overstuffed armchair and a cheap spinet piano. A huge, unabridged dictionary sits on a brass book-stand near the piano.*

SCENE ONE

AT THE CURTAIN:
NATHAN *is sitting on the couch, reading a book.* ELEANOR *is sewing.* MAGGIE *is studying* NATHAN *and sketching him with charcoal on a large pad.* NATHAN *occasionally glances at* MAGGIE *with an expression that increasingly suggests impatience.*

NATHAN. Maggie? (MAGGIE *doesn't respond.*) Maggie?

MAGGIE. (*after a long beat, still drawing*) Mmmmm?

147

NATHAN. It's time to stop pretending.

MAGGIE. Pretending?

NATHAN. Why not try needlepoint? Or maybe crocheting.

MAGGIE. I'm definitely getting better.

NATHAN. You are?

MAGGIE. I am.

ELEANOR. There. Your blouse is as good as new.

MAGGIE. What do you think, Mom?

ELEANOR. I'm sorry, I didn't hear you.

MAGGIE. (*petulantly*) Don't you think I'm becoming a better artist?

ELEANOR. There's no reason to get angry.

MAGGIE. Grandpa says I'm not an artist. And I never will be.

ELEANOR. He's usually right about things like that.

MAGGIE. Thanks for boosting my ego.

ELEANOR. I'm sorry, dear. I know nothing about art.

NATHAN. At least you admit it.

ELEANOR. It's hard enough for me to learn a little bit about music. We all have our parts to play, you know.

NATHAN. Was that a *play* on words, Eleanor?

ELEANOR. (*puzzled*) I don't think so.

MAGGIE. My drawings are getting better.

NATHAN. Because you *say* they are?

MAGGIE. I want to be an artist. Why won't you let me?

NATHAN. It's not who you are. I didn't decide that. We *all* did.

MAGGIE. We can change. *I've* changed.

NATHAN. Do you even know what the word "art" means?

MAGGIE. Please, not today. School's out.

NATHAN. We never stop learning.

MAGGIE. I just want to draw a few lousy pictures.

NATHAN. In that case, "mission accomplished."

ELEANOR. Listen to Grandpa, dear.

MAGGIE. Don't I always?

NATHAN. Let's talk about art, Maggie.

MAGGIE. (*muttering to herself*) A few lousy pictures...

NATHAN. Do you see this book?

MAGGIE. I hope they didn't charge you by the pound.

ELEANOR. Be serious, dear.

NATHAN. It's *The Decline and Fall of the Roman Empire*.

MAGGIE. There goes the surprise ending.

NATHAN. It's a frightening story. A great civilization under attack, under siege, and finally destroyed by barbarians.

MAGGIE. There are *always* barbarians.

ELEANOR. We're safe here.

MAGGIE. They can't touch us.

NATHAN. This book is a great work of art.

MAGGIE. Damn! I thought I was out of the woods.

NATHAN. What is art, Maggie?

MAGGIE. No sense wasting time. (*She walks to the dictionary, leafs through the pages, finds the word. Reads wearily.*) "Art. The quality, production, expression, or realm, according to aesthetic principles, of what is beautiful, appealing, or of more than ordinary significance."

NATHAN. Aesthetic principles.

ELEANOR. Beauty.

NATHAN. And art demands discipline, too. But discipline isn't enough.

ELEANOR. You need talent.

MAGGIE. No shit.

NATHAN. And if you don't have talent—and take my word for it, you *don't--*

MAGGIE. You're really a nasty old bastard.

ELEANOR. Maggie, you shouldn't...

MAGGIE. If you weren't my grandfather...

NATHAN. I'd be someone *else's* grandfather, wouldn't I?

MAGGIE. I didn't—

NATHAN. Is that what you want?

MAGGIE. No.

NATHAN. Are you sure about that?

MAGGIE. I'm sorry. I guess I'm getting a little stir crazy.

ELEANOR. Me, too, Pa.

MAGGIE. We're all feeling it.

ELEANOR. We're not—*complete* any more.

NATHAN. What do you want me to do, Eleanor?

ELEANOR. I don't know.

NATHAN. I'm not God. I can't grab a handful of dirt and breathe life into it.

MAGGIE. You know how long it's been since I got laid?

ELEANOR. I'm afraid we do. You've been telling us about it every day.

NATHAN. We must be patient.

ELEANOR. Patient.

MAGGIE. We've got to get lucky. Soon.

NATHAN. It's happened before.

ELEANOR. Daniel's always on the look-out, God bless him. Always "taking care of our problems."

MAGGIE. I wonder what's keeping Daddy.

ELEANOR. He needs time by himself.

MAGGIE. Wandering around in the woods? You've seen one tree, you've seen them all.

NATHAN. There's nothing noble about Nature. It's kill or be killed.

MAGGIE. Amen to that.

ELEANOR. For Daniel, it was always different. When we lived in the city, if he had a spare hour, he would be off to the park.

MAGGIE. At least he's willing to do what *I* won't do. Go out there again—to the store—to the post office.

NATHAN. Out among the barbarians.

ELEANOR. I can't do it anymore, either. Where would we be...?

NATHAN. He'll get to the market. Eventually.

MAGGIE. Not until he takes some more of those great candid photos--of animals running like hell to get away from him.

ELEANOR. The pictures don't matter to him. It's being out in the woods. The smell of the grass and the wildflowers. He's at peace.

MAGGIE. Maybe he's hitting on a moose. Or does he even think about things like that any more?

NATHAN. Did he ever?

ELEANOR. Of course he did. But we're not about that now.

MAGGIE. When Jonathan was here—when he was writing those love poems to you—

NATHAN. Awful, amateurish stuff!

MAGGIE. Daddy was never jealous?

ELEANOR. Never.

MAGGIE. Did you want him to be?

ELEANOR. No. He understood.

MAGGIE. I thought you were hot for Jonathan. You called it "romance."

NATHAN. She was just trying to remember being young.

MAGGIE. You miss Jonathan a lot, don't you, Mom?

ELEANOR. I cared about him.

MAGGIE. You're sure he didn't turn you on?

ELEANOR. Positive. But he pleased me.

NATHAN. It doesn't matter. Jonathan is the past.

MAGGIE. I wish he wasn't. Maybe we pushed him too hard.

ELEANOR. As Grandpa says, that's the past.

NATHAN. It's almost a quarter to six, Eleanor. Dinner won't be late, will it?

MAGGIE. Chop-chop, Momma. Let's keep Grandpa happy. That's your job, right?

(ELEANOR *exits to kitchen. Sound of approaching automobile. Two car doors slam shut.*)

NATHAN. The prodigal father returns.

(DANIEL *enters, carrying grocery bags. He is followed by* ADAM, *who is wearing a backpack.*)

DANIEL. Grandpa, Maggie. Look what I brought home for dinner.

ADAM. Hello.

MAGGIE. Is he our guest, Daddy—or the main course?

DANIEL. Careful, Maggie. He might take you seriously.

ADAM. I guess you weren't kidding when you said this place was off the beaten track.

MAGGIE. (*She walks around* ADAM, *inspecting him carefully, looking him up and down.*) Where'd you find him?

DANIEL. At the market. He said he needed a ride. And he thought he might help me do some work around here, too.

ADAM. If the price is right.

DANIEL. He looked like he could use a good, hot meal.

ADAM. I'm not as desperate as all that. My name is Adam.

NATHAN. Nice to meet you, Adam.

MAGGIE. You do look a little wasted. Had anything to eat lately?

ADAM. When I'm hungry, I eat.

NATHAN. Where are you headed, son?

ADAM. Boston. I hope you can get there from here.

MAGGIE. You can, if you're lucky.

ADAM. I didn't expect to end up out in the woods.

MAGGIE. You should be more careful when you hitch a ride.

ADAM. I'll write that down in my book of "do's" and "don't's." You like it out here?

NATHAN. We enjoy our privacy.

DANIEL. Don't worry. I'll take you back to the highway whenever you decide to leave.

ADAM. (*confidently*) I'm not worried.

NATHAN. Where are you from?

ADAM. Lexington, Mass, originally.

MAGGIE. What about *lately*?

ADAM. I've been traveling, picking up work. Making a few bucks and moving on. I'm saving up for a gypsy wagon.

ELEANOR. (*enters*) What have we here?

DANIEL. Adam, this is my wife, Eleanor. Our daughter, Maggie. And this is Eleanor's father, Nathan. We usually call him "Grandpa."

ADAM. Nice to meet you.

DANIEL. Can I help you take that load off your back?

ADAM. (*He pulls away quickly, avoiding* DANIEL's *touch.*) No, that's okay.

(*He takes off the backpack, then stands near the entrance, the backpack at his feet.*)

ELEANOR. Dinner's on the stove. My beef stew. You'll love it.

DANIEL. It's the best ever. The meat melts in your mouth.

ELEANOR. Tender baby carrots.

NATHAN. Just the right touch of spices.

MAGGIE. She's got a heavy hand with the garlic.

ADAM. I'm into garlic. Sounds tempting.

ELEANOR. Then don't hesitate. Give in.

NATHAN. What's waiting for you in Boston?

MAGGIE. A woman, I'll bet.

ADAM. I never know what's waiting for me. Do you? (*long beat*) I'll find out when I get there.

ELEANOR. I hope you can stay with us for a few days.

ADAM. I *am* short of cash.

NATHAN. Daniel needs a lot of help.

DANIEL. Sure do. I've got to take off the old molding in here...

NATHAN. And replace it.

ELEANOR. The kitchen needs repainting.

MAGGIE. And all three of the bedrooms.

DANIEL. The staircase needs fixing, too.

NATHAN. And I'm in no shape to help.

ADAM. That's a long list. I might have to join the carpenter's union.

DANIEL. We'll make it worth your while.

ADAM. I'm listening.

DANIEL. How does twenty-five dollars a day sound?

ADAM. Well...

DANIEL. Plus, like we used to say in the army, "three hots and a cot."

ELEANOR. Baked ham. Potato dumplings, light as a feather. Rice pudding, filled with plump, juicy raisins. Dutch apple pie.

ADAM. You should be writing TV commercials.

NATHAN. You can sleep on the couch.

DANIEL. It's very comfortable. I fall asleep there all the time.

MAGGIE. And after "lights out", who knows?

DANIEL. What do you say, Adam?

ADAM. Maybe.

MAGGIE. It's just for a couple of days. We're not adopting you.

DANIEL. (*laughing a little too loudly*) But we haven't ruled that out yet!

(*No one else joins in the laughter, which ends abruptly.*)

NATHAN. It's up to you.

(ADAM *walks to the overstuffed chair, and sits in it. It engulfs him.*)

DANIEL. (*laughing again*) That chair'll eat you alive, if you don't watch out!

(MAGGIE *sits on the floor at the foot of the chair.* DANIEL *positions himself behind the chair, looking down at* ADAM. ELEANOR *stands just behind* MAGGIE.)

ADAM. Why do you live so far out in the woods?

NATHAN. I told you, we're private people.

MAGGIE. You could be murdered out here, and no one would hear you screaming.

DANIEL. Maggie!

ELEANOR. My daughter has a strange sense of humor. God knows where she got it. Certainly not from me.

MAGGIE. (*She begins sketching* ADAM.) Yeah, Mom's about as funny as gangrene.

DANIEL. How long have you been..."traveling around"?

ADAM. A couple of years.

NATHAN. Did you go to college?

ADAM. UMass. But I didn't graduate. My father died. I ran out of money.

MAGGIE. I know the feeling.

DANIEL. *We're* doing fine.

MAGGIE. We are, huh?

ELEANOR. Grandpa has his pension.

NATHAN. And my social security.

DANIEL. We managed to put aside some money, too.

ADAM. Doesn't sound like much.

DANIEL. We're doing fine.

ELEANOR. Most important of all, we have each other.

DANIEL. And we're kind of self-sufficient.

MAGGIE. We have a big vegetable garden out back—tomatoes, lettuce, zucchini, eggplant, cucumber.

NATHAN. Eleanor and Maggie are the farmers.

DANIEL. I help them out with the chores.

ELEANOR. We've even got half a dozen hens.

NATHAN. Fresh eggs!

MAGGIE. And plenty of chickenshit for fertilizer.

DANIEL. There are three apple trees, too. And we raise strawberries and blueberries.

ADAM. Where do you keep the cows?

MAGGIE. Please, don't give them any ideas. I'm not the milk-maid type.

ADAM. Sounds like hard work.

ELEANOR. It is.

DANIEL. But we can take care of ourselves.

MAGGIE. And if we ever get snowbound, we can eat each other.

ELEANOR. What was your major in college, Adam?

ADAM. History.

NATHAN. My favorite subject. I'm re-reading Gibbons' *Decline and Fall* again. Have you read it?

ADAM. Yes, I have.

NATHAN. Marvelous piece of work, isn't it?

ADAM. Too long-winded for me. Too much Greek and Latin in the footnotes. *Delenda est Carthago!*

NATHAN. But what a marvelous canvas he paints!

ADAM. He blames everything on the Christians and the barbarians, right?

NATHAN. I suppose so.

ADAM. But the Romans *became* Christians, and they *hired* the barbarians, didn't they? I'd say the Romans brought it all on themselves.

MAGGIE. I'm waiting for the Reader's Digest version.

NATHAN. What was your specialty? Ancient civilization? Modern European?

ADAM. American history.

MAGGIE. How patriotic.

(*She sings a few lines from "God Bless America."*)

ELEANOR. Ever thought about going back to get your degree?

ADAM. I might.

DANIEL. How do you plan to make a living?

NATHAN. Do you have any special talent?

ELEANOR. Any special skill?

NATHAN. Would you like to teach history?

ADAM. What is this, a quiz show?

DANIEL. We're just making conversation.

ADAM. I haven't made up my mind about school. I've got time.

MAGGIE. How old are you, Adam?

ADAM. Twenty-five.

ELEANOR. I suddenly feel ancient. (*Touching* ADAM's *shoulder lightly, she starts toward the kitchen.*) Stay for dinner, dear. Please. For *me.*

(She exits.)

NATHAN. I understand, Adam. A young man has a lot of options. It isn't easy to choose the right one.

ADAM. I never worry about making choices. I like to let things just happen.

DANIEL. Really?

MAGGIE. (*Holds up her sketch of* ADAM *so he can see it.*) This still needs a lot of work, but...

ADAM. That's pretty good. I recognize me.

NATHAN. She *tries.*

ADAM. Can I have it when you're finished?

MAGGIE. Sure. I'll even sign it. It may be worth a fortune some day.

ELEANOR. (*enters*) Dinner will be ready in a few minutes.

ADAM. (*rising*) I'm kind of dusty from the road. I'd like to clean up. Change my shirt. Can you point me toward the bathroom?

ELEANOR. Down the hall, first door on the left. I've already hung a clean towel on the rack above the sink.

ADAM. Thanks.

(*He exits into the hall, carrying his backpack.*)

DANIEL. When he hitched a ride—

(ELEANOR *gestures for him to stop talking, checks that the bathroom door is closed, then nods to* DANIEL.)

DANIEL. He never asked me where I was going. That's kind of odd, isn't it?

NATHAN. He just got into the car with you?

DANIEL. I didn't even have to go into my sales pitch.

MAGGIE. I don't think he's afraid of you, Daddy. Or anyone else.

ELEANOR. His eyes are very...soulful. He's quite interesting.

DANIEL. He needs the money. He'll stay.

MAGGIE. I hope so.

ELEANOR. So do I.

NATHAN. Are we certain we want him to stay?

DANIEL. Why not?

MAGGIE. He's so young.

NATHAN. Maybe for a week or so? See if he fits in?

DANIEL. Yes, a week or so.

ELEANOR. Maggie, help me set the table. (*As* MAGGIE *and* ELEANOR *begin to set the table*, ADAM *enters*.) Feel a little more human?

ADAM. Sure do. I'll stay for dinner. And I'll work on the house with you tomorrow.

DANIEL. And maybe a few days longer?

ADAM. Maybe.

DANIEL. Suppose we up the ante? How about thirty dollars a day?

ADAM. Make it thirty-*five*.

NATHAN. Isn't that a little steep?

DANIEL. No, thirty-five is okay. It's fair. We can do it.

ADAM. Let me think about it.

DANIEL. Take your time.

ADAM. (*To* NATHAN) You mind if I ask you something?

NATHAN. After our little "quiz show?" It's only fair.

ADAM. What did you do for a living?

NATHAN. I was a teacher. Taught English Literature in college. Retired a few years ago.

ADAM. Where did you teach?

NATHAN. A small school out in the Midwest, in Ohio. Stratfield College.

ADAM. Never heard of it. You liked teaching?

NATHAN. Loved it. Books were my whole life.

ELEANOR. They still are.

NATHAN. But my health went downhill. My heart's a little weak.

ELEANOR. So he retired.

DANIEL. And he moved out here to live with us.

NATHAN. I have a passion for books. A love for teaching. It was difficult to give it up. But I no longer had the energy to do right by my students. *(after a beat)* You'll find your passion, believe me. We all do.

ADAM. *(to DANIEL)* Are *you* still working?

DANIEL. None of us are.

MAGGIE. We all retired together—one big, happy family.

ADAM. *All* of you?

DANIEL. We decided, together, as a family, to do this.

ADAM. To do *what*?

NATHAN. To live as far from other people as we can, at least for a while.

ADAM. Why?

DANIEL. It's our way to take time out.

MAGGIE. To recharge our batteries.

ELEANOR. To catch up on things.

ADAM. Like feeding the hens?

DANIEL. We help each other, encourage each other.

ELEANOR. For me, it's the piano. I played a little, when I was young.

DANIEL. But you never had a chance to get good at it, did you, sweetheart?

ELEANOR. I've been practicing. Working hard. Trying hard. I'm getting better, a little at a time.

DANIEL. You should play for Adam later.

ELEANOR. Maybe I will, dear.

DANIEL. Me? I like to go fishing. Sit by the lake and watch the clouds drift by. And daydream.

MAGGIE. He even catches a fish, once in a while.

DANIEL. Sometimes I "hunt"—with a camera, of course. I'm not a killer. You should come out with me, Adam. I'd like the company. It's so peaceful in the woods.

MAGGIE. I think Daddy's beginning to develop roots. When he dies, we won't have to bury him. We'll just plant him somewhere.

NATHAN. I've had more time to study, to read the great books again. There's never enough time for the great books, is there?

ELEANOR. And you're writing, too, aren't you, Pa?

NATHAN. A survey of the modern novel. Nothing I'm ready to show anyone yet.

ADAM. I've never had any patience for criticism. Who cares what anyone else thinks about a book?

MAGGIE. I want to be an artist, but I've got nobody to teach me. Maybe I'm not good enough anyway. The jury's still out... Grandpa thinks I'm hopeless.

ADAM. I like the drawing you did of me.

MAGGIE. Thanks. But I gotta tell you, for me, this place gets—lonely. So I curl up with a nice bottle of wine...

DANIEL. Maggie tends to exaggerate.

ELEANOR. But she's right.

DANIEL. Our little corner of the world isn't perfect.

ELEANOR. But it's *our* world.

DANIEL. We make the rules. Live the way we want to live.

ELEANOR. Maybe, with us, you'll find out how *you* want to live.

ADAM. I *know* how I want to live.

DANIEL. We understand how you feel.

ADAM. Do you?

NATHAN. I think we do.

ADAM. You don't know me at all.

ELEANOR. Then let us *get* to know you.

ADAM. I'll stay for a couple of days. Let's leave it at that.

DANIEL. Okay.

ADAM. And for thirty-five dollars a day, you've got yourself a handyman.

NATHAN. This calls for a drink.

MAGGIE. I second the motion.

ELEANOR. Daniel, why don't you do the honors?

DANIEL. (*Nods agreement. Goes to the cabinet, takes out two bottles of wine. Shows them to NATHAN.*) What should I pour this evening?

NATHAN. Well, considering what's for dinner, a Bordeaux would be appropriate.

(DANIEL *returns one bottle to the cabinet, fills five glasses from the other bottle and distributes them. Raises his glass.*)

DANIEL. To your health, Adam.

(NATHAN and MAGGIE *raise their glasses and echo "To your health, Adam." ADAM raises his glass and they all drink.*)

DANIEL. So you'll stay for a few days and help me do the work.

ELEANOR. There'll be plenty of good food.

NATHAN. And maybe a fresh look for this place.

DANIEL. We had another young man stay with us for a while.

MAGGIE. (*Softly, tenderly*) Jonathan.

ELEANOR. He loved my baked ham.

NATHAN. While he was here, he started writing a book. A novel. Have you ever been interested in writing, Adam?

ADAM. No. When I was a kid, I used to make up stories sometimes. But I never wrote them down.

ELEANOR. Did you ever tell the stories to your friends?

ADAM. No. I didn't want to share them. When I was alone, out in the back yard, or waiting for the school bus in the morning, I made believe I was someone else—a cowboy, a mountain climber, an explorer. It made the time pass.

DANIEL. There's nothing wrong with daydreams.

ELEANOR. Dinner should be ready. Maggie, would you help me serve?

MAGGIE. I wouldn't miss it for the world.

(ELEANOR *and* MAGGIE *exit.* NATHAN, DANIEL *and* ADAM *sit at the table. They beckon* ADAM *to sit between them, facing the audience.*)

NATHAN. We're glad you'll be spending some time with us.

DANIEL. Yeah, I sure can use another pair of hands.

ADAM. I can use the money.

DANIEL. I guess you're in the right place at the right time.

(ELEANOR *and* MAGGIE *enter with platters of food and place them on the table. They sit down.*)

NATHAN. Let us say Grace.

(*They join hands around the table,* NATHAN *and* DANIEL *grasping* ADAM's *hands.*)

Dear Lord, for the joys of our family, our home, our hearth, and for the added joy of bringing a new friend, Adam, to join us and share this place with us, and for the blessing of this food, we thank Thee with all our hearts.

ALL. (*except* ADAM.) Amen.

(ADAM *moves to detach his hands, but neither* NATHAN *nor* DANIEL *releases them. Everyone is staring at* ADAM. *He is unable to free his hands. Everyone continues to stare at him. Finally,* ADAM *says "Amen."* NATHAN *and* DANIEL *release his hands. Everyone smiles.*)

END OF SCENE ONE

SCENE TWO

TIME:
Late that night.

AT THE CURTAIN:
ADAM *is sitting on the couch, alone in the room, his backpack at his feet. There is a blanket and pillow on the couch. The room is dark, except for the light of a nearby lamp. He takes off his shirt, folds it carefully and puts it on the chair. He switches off the lamp, lies down on the couch. After two or three long beats,* MAGGIE *enters from the hallway, carrying a glass of wine.*

MAGGIE. Hey, Adam. Aaah-dam. Come on, you're not asleep.

ADAM. Yes, I am.

MAGGIE. (*She tickles him. He pushes her away. She switches on the lamp.*) Move over. Give me some room.

ADAM. You're drinking?

MAGGIE. Of course I am. But drinking alone isn't healthy. You'd better join me.

ADAM. In the middle of the night? No, thanks.

MAGGIE. Let me pass along a valuable lesson I've learned: the best way to avoid a hangover is just to keep on drinking.

ADAM. I'm tired.

MAGGIE. From what? Your after-dinner walk in the woods with Smokey the Bear? Boring, yes. Tiring, no. Then a long talk with Grandpa—a lot of literary crap—the decline and fall of practically everything. Of course, you didn't care about any of it. Nobody does. And you listened politely to Mamma's pathetic attempt to play the piano. You call that a full day? Come on, boy.

ADAM. I'm not a boy.

(MAGGIE *caresses his face, runs her fingers through his hair, kisses his mouth. He pulls away from her.*)

MAGGIE. You kiss like a boy. Or maybe it's boys you *like* to kiss. Is that it?

ADAM. It's *sleep* that I like.

MAGGIE. (*She takes his hand and presses it against her breast.*) Okay, maybe this isn't Mount Everest. But it ain't Death Valley, either. (*She lets go of his hand. He keeps pressing it against her breast.*) That's progress, I guess.

(ADAM *leans forward suddenly, embraces her roughly and kisses her. He pulls back, still holding her close, caressing her breasts, her thighs.*)

MAGGIE. Hey, take it easy. Try a little tenderness.

ADAM. I'm not romantic about sex.

MAGGIE. But you don't have to break my arm!

ADAM. I guess you're not as tough as you look.

MAGGIE. Do I look tough?

ADAM. You like to *think* you do.

MAGGIE. You're pulling my chain already. And you hardly know me.

ADAM. Everybody here is pulling *my* chain.

MAGGIE. No, we're not.

ADAM. Your family's way off base.

MAGGIE. What family isn't?

ADAM. You're all afraid of Nathan.

MAGGIE. That's not true.

ADAM. You keep asking him for permission.

MAGGIE. We love him.

ADAM. He's the boss.

MAGGIE. That's what we want him to be.

ADAM. When he prays, you'd better say "Amen"...

MAGGIE. Because he taught us our prayers.

ADAM. Ah, yes, the noble professor. (*He kisses* MAGGIE, *opens the buttons of her blouse, pulls it off, folds it neatly and puts it down.*) And the vengeful God of the house.

MAGGIE. He's just my grandfather.

ADAM. Why did that other guy—what was his name?

MAGGIE. Jonathan.

ADAM. Why did he leave?

MAGGIE. We don't know.

ADAM. Did Nathan tell him to go?

MAGGIE. No.

ADAM. You sure about that?

MAGGIE. He and Jonathan were very close. But they argued all the time.

ADAM. About what?

MAGGIE. Do you call this "foreplay?"

ADAM. What did they argue about?

MAGGIE. Jonathan's novel.

ADAM. Go on.

MAGGIE. Go on?

ADAM. Why were they arguing about the novel?

MAGGIE. Jonathan wanted to write it his way. Grandpa kept telling him to change it.

ADAM. Is that why Jonathan left?

MAGGIE. Beats me.

ADAM. How long was he here?

MAGGIE. About as long as it's taking you to get it on with me. Almost a year. He left six, seven months ago. Can we get back to business now?

(*As the action proceeds*, ELEANOR *enters and stands unseen in the darkness by* ADAM *and* MAGGIE.)

ADAM. What about *you*, Maggie?

MAGGIE. What *about* me?

ADAM. Why do you want to live way the hell out here, so far away from everything?

MAGGIE. I'll be glad to tell you my whole life story—after I get laid.

ADAM. If you're lonely, why do you stay here?

MAGGIE. Please...

ADAM. You're too young to waste your time in the middle of nowhere.

MAGGIE. I'm getting older by the minute. (*after a beat*) We're family, Adam. I need that. I was a lot lonelier before.

ADAM. Were you ever married?

MAGGIE. (*impatiently*) Adam...

ADAM. Were you?

MAGGIE. When I was twenty. Divorced, when I was twenty-five.

ADAM. What was his name?

MAGGIE. (*in a smaller, less aggressive voice*) Christian. I called him Christy. (*In that same voice, her eyes closed as she speaks, she begins to respond to* ADAM's *caresses.*) He was handsome. Almost pretty. Much prettier than me. Everyone said so. I met him in college.

ADAM. You got married while you were still in school?

MAGGIE. Yes.

ADAM. It didn't work out.

MAGGIE. (*pulling away from him*) You know, you're not playing your cards right.

ADAM. Did *you* leave *him*, or did *he* leave *you*?

MAGGIE. I don't remember. It was a long time ago.

ADAM. You remember.

MAGGIE. You're a boring little bastard.

ADAM. What happened?

MAGGIE. Christy wanted too much from me.

ADAM. Too much *what*?

MAGGIE. Too much love.

ADAM. Didn't you love him?

MAGGIE. Yes. But not the way *he* loved *me*.

ADAM. What do you mean?

MAGGIE. He didn't hide anything from me. His fears. His anger. If he said something that hurt me, he never apologized. He said that honesty was the best part of love.

ADAM. Honesty...

MAGGIE. It scared me.

ADAM. So he left you.

MAGGIE. No, *I* left *him*.

ADAM. Poor Maggie.

MAGGIE. Sometimes he made me feel—I don't know—like I wasn't even a person.

ADAM. Poor, poor Maggie.

MAGGIE. How can anyone love that way?

(*As the action proceeds, DANIEL enters, stands watching MAGGIE and ADAM for several beats. Then he takes ELEANOR's hand, kisses it. They kiss, embrace passionately. They exit together.*)

ADAM. (*becoming more passionate, kissing MAGGIE, caressing her*) You don't have to love *me*. *I* don't even love me.

MAGGIE. (*pushing him away, standing up, in her customary hard-edged voice*) No, no. Too late. No nookie for you tonight.

ADAM. (*pulling her back onto the couch*) Come on, Maggie. Come to poppa.

(*She hesitates, then responds to him, kisses him, touches his thigh, his calf. She pulls away.*)

MAGGIE. What the hell is *that*?

(ADAM *pulls up one leg of his jeans, revealing a hunting knife in a scabbard fastened around his ankle.*)

ADAM. You never know who you run into on the road. This is my pacifier. It helps me fall asleep.

MAGGIE. It's kind of a turn-on.

ADAM. Whatever works for you.

MAGGIE. No more questions?

ADAM. No more questions.

(As ADAM *and* MAGGIE *begin to make love, she switches off the lamp.)*
ADAM. In the dark? Because it's me?

MAGGIE. No. Because it's *me.*

END OF SCENE TWO

SCENE THREE

TIME:
A couple of minutes later.

AT THE CURTAIN:
DANIEL *and* ELEANOR *enter their bedroom, holding hands.*

ELEANOR. I wish Maggie was better at loving.

DANIEL. And lying.

ELEANOR. Like us?

DANIEL. *(embracing her)* We're better at loving, too, aren't we?

ELEANOR. *(Kisses him.)* Yes, my darling.

DANIEL. I wonder about Adam.

ELEANOR. Maybe Maggie's right.

DANIEL. What did she say?

ELEANOR. That he isn't afraid of anyone.

DANIEL. He does seem awfully sure of himself.

ELEANOR. Too sure to be one of us?

DANIEL. Don't worry, sweetheart. I can take care of any problem we have with him.

ELEANOR. I know, dear.

DANIEL. Don't fret about it, okay?

ELEANOR. We don't need more problems.

DANIEL. That's right. No more problems.

ELEANOR. We've had enough.

DANIEL. You'll always be safe with me, sweetheart. I'll take care of you.

ELEANOR. Like you always have.

DANIEL. Like I always have.

ELEANOR. I'm surprised Maggie has stayed with us.

DANIEL. I'm not.

ELEANOR. She's afraid, like the rest of us. But she's a young woman. I have you, Daniel. We have each other. When Jonathan left...

DANIEL. She needs love.

ELEANOR. That's true, but...

DANIEL. It's *your* love she needs. More than Jonathan's. Or Adam's. Or mine.

ELEANOR. I guess she does.

DANIEL. That's why she came with us. That's why she stayed. She needs her mother.

ELEANOR. Even though her "mother" is a sinner? Of course, she doesn't know that.

DANIEL. You didn't do anything wrong.

ELEANOR. There are some things you can't protect me from.

DANIEL. Sweetheart, you're not guilty of anything.

ELEANOR. It's not *your* secret, Daniel, it's *ours*.

DANIEL. But it's not your *sin*.

ELEANOR. I had a dream a couple of nights ago. It really scared me.

DANIEL. A nightmare?

ELEANOR. Yes. I was living back in Hartford, but I was alone. I was sitting in a rocking chair, in a small, narrow room with big mirrors on all the walls. Everywhere I looked, I could see myself. I was old. And I was alone. I had always been alone. I had never met you.

DANIEL. (*He embraces her.*) It was only a dream. You're not alone, sweetheart.

ELEANOR. I was. For so long. I had given up hope.

DANIEL. Me, too. But we met, didn't we? We fell in love.

ELEANOR. We're *still* in love, aren't we?

DANIEL. Yes. And we always *will* be.

ELEANOR. Always.

DANIEL. (*smiling*) Now, if only I could play the piano.

ELEANOR. Then you'd be absolutely perfect!

DANIEL. You mean, I'm *not* perfect?

ELEANOR. Of course you are.

DANIEL. (*tenderly*) I understand. You want to play as well as your mother did.

ELEANOR. She loved her music so much.

DANIEL. I wish I could help you, sweetheart. But I'm famous for my tin ear. *Two* tin ears!

ELEANOR. I think—I believe—that music is *in* me, Daniel. Is a part of me.

DANIEL. I believe that, too. And, tin ear and all, you'll always be the music in my life.

ELEANOR. (*laughs*) From someone who's tone-deaf, I'm not so sure that's a compliment.

(DANIEL *laughs. They kiss.*)

END OF SCENE THREE

SCENE FOUR

TIME:
Two weeks later, just before noon.

AT THE CURTAIN:
There have been some changes in the living room-dining room: a trunk stands on the floor alongside the couch. ADAM's backpack rests on the lid of the trunk. A coat rack stands near the trunk. On the coat rack, on hangars, are ADAM's windbreaker, two or three shirts, and a pair of slacks. Two drawings, one of ADAM, one of NATHAN, have been hung on the wall. A large photograph of a deer rests on the mantel. A tool kit stands against the back wall.

NATHAN *is reading.* ELEANOR *is seated at the piano, studying a piece of music, practicing her fingering without playing.* MAGGIE *is drinking wine and working on a sketch.*

MAGGIE. I can't believe Adam spends so much time with Daddy.

NATHAN. It's rather ridiculous.

ELEANOR. You've got nothing to complain about, Maggie.

MAGGIE. I know, I know.

ELEANOR. Why are you still drinking so much?

MAGGIE. Before Adam, I was compensating. Now, I'm celebrating.

NATHAN. Well at least *some* of us are happy.

ELEANOR. He's not what I thought he would be.

MAGGIE. You mean "those soulful eyes"?

ELEANOR. And yet there are times when I look at him...

MAGGIE. You're dreaming, Mamma.

ELEANOR. There's nothing wrong with that.

MAGGIE. Be careful.

ELEANOR. There *is* a kind of tenderness...

MAGGIE. No way.

ELEANOR. Just because he isn't tender with *you*...

NATHAN. Eleanor, don't be foolish.

ELEANOR. He's only been with us for a couple of weeks. We don't—

NATHAN. He isn't Jonathan. He isn't what we need.

MAGGIE. No pretty love poems.

NATHAN. Smart, but very little intellectual curiosity. I don't find him particularly interesting.

MAGGIE. Speak for yourself, Grandpa.

NATHAN. I'm trying to speak for all of us. I guess I can't do that any more.

MAGGIE. I'll put in a good word for you.

NATHAN. When I need your help, I'll be sure to ask for it.

ELEANOR. He's actually taught Daniel how to use that camera.

MAGGIE. Yes. He's been taking some pretty good pictures.

NATHAN. Just what we needed. A wildlife photographer.

(*The front door opens.* DANIEL *and* ADAM *enter.*)

MAGGIE. Speaking of wild life...

DANIEL. What a beautiful morning! I worked up a hell of an appetite out there.

ELEANOR. I get the message. I'll make lunch in a couple of minutes, dear.

MAGGIE. How about you, Adam? Hungry for anything?

NATHAN. Lord preserve us.

ADAM. What are you working on, Eleanor?

ELEANOR. A Chopin etude. (ADAM *goes to the piano, looks over* ELEANOR's *shoulder at the music.*) I can imagine it, but I can't make it happen.

ADAM. Let me hear the first couple of bars.

ELEANOR. I'm not really—I haven't practiced...

ADAM. (*He sits down beside her, very close to her.*) Just a few bars.

ELEANOR. I have to make lunch.

DANIEL. Go ahead and play, sweetheart. He won't bite you.

MAGGIE. Don't be so sure.

(DANIEL *watches* ADAM *and* ELEANOR *for a moment, then goes to stand behind them.*)

ELEANOR. Just a few bars– (*She haltingly plays the opening of Chopin's Etude in E major, Opus 10 #3 –"Tristesse." She struggles, hits a few wrong notes, stops playing.*) I told you. I can't—

(*She rises, tries to leave the piano.* ADAM *takes her arm, preventing her from leaving.*)

ADAM. Don't run away, Eleanor. I'll tell you the secret to playing Chopin. I learned it a long time ago.

(DANIEL *puts his hands on* ELEANOR's *shoulders, reminding her of his presence.*)

ELEANOR. The secret?

ADAM. Whatever the tempo—keep the beat in your left hand, and change the flow in your right. Steal a beat here—and add it there.

(*He plays the opening of the Etude, beautifully, skillfully.*)

NATHAN. That's called "rubato." It *means* stolen.

ADAM. Steal some time here. Add it there.

(*He stops playing.*)

DANIEL. (*He massages* ELEANOR's *shoulders.*) Nice. Very nice.

ELEANOR. Don't stop playing.

ADAM. *You* try it. (*He plays a few bars.*) Go ahead.

(*She tries to imitate his phrasing. She has some success.*)

ELEANOR. Yes. I see.

DANIEL. (*jealously, with counterfeit enthusiasm*) Atta girl!

ADAM. Good. Keep working on it.

NATHAN. (*to* ADAM) You're not quite what you seem to be, are you?

ADAM. I'm exactly what I seem to be, Nathan. Not what you'd *like* me to be.

MAGGIE. Grandpa wants you to be a writer.

ADAM. From what I hear, Jonathan didn't exactly fill the bill, either.

NATHAN. He had genuine talent.

ADAM. But not enough?

NATHAN. We often disagreed. The traditional tension between authors and critics.

ELEANOR. They both enjoyed those arguments.

ADAM. I'm not interested in his book. Or is it *yours*?

NATHAN. I never wrote a single word. He did it all. I reacted, made suggestions, tried to give him the benefit of my knowledge and experience.

ADAM. I've told you, I'm not a writer.

NATHAN. I'd be interested in your opinion.

ADAM. It wouldn't be worth much.

DANIEL. I tried to read that damn book. Couldn't finish it. It was about a kid—a teenager, who runs away from home.

ELEANOR. It was too complicated for me.

MAGGIE. (*with a hint of sarcasm*) Thank God for your music, Mamma!

ADAM. As I said, I'm not a writer.

NATHAN. You never know.

ADAM. I know who I am.

NATHAN. Maybe, if you give yourself a chance...

ADAM. I'm not Jonathan. I don't need your help to be me.

NATHAN. He was just someone who lived with us for a while.

ADAM. I won't be here that long.

MAGGIE. I remember those fights about the book.

ELEANOR. Me, too.

DANIEL. Knock-down drag-outs!

(MAGGIE *and* ELEANOR *act out the following "dialogue." * MAGGIE *plays* NATHAN, *using a deep, authoritative voice.*)

MAGGIE. "Jonathan, that scene is ridiculous! Eighteen-year-old boys don't talk that way."

ELEANOR. "*He* does."

MAGGIE. "He sounds just like *you!*"

ELEANOR. "I made him up, didn't I? He can be anything I want him to be!"

MAGGIE. "My boy, you still have so much to learn."

NATHAN. (*softly*) Please, no more.

ELEANOR. Jonathan was no pushover.

DANIEL. He hated to give in.

ELEANOR. He never won.

MAGGIE. But he made Grandpa *work* for it.

NATHAN. Don't be so dramatic. I did what teachers do. That's not always appreciated.

DANIEL. (*proud of his ability to remember*) It was called *Family Ties!*

ADAM. I thought you said it was about a kid who ran away from home. Why would he call it *Family Ties?*

NATHAN. The title is ironic. Do you know what irony is, Adam?

ADAM. I think I do.

MAGGIE. Uh-oh! Dictionary time.

NATHAN. Adam, see that big dictionary over there? I want you to go to it, and look up the word "irony." I-r-o-n-y. Go ahead.

ADAM. You've got to be kidding.

NATHAN. I'm not.

ADAM. I *know* what it means.

NATHAN. Do me a favor and look it up.

(ADAM *hesitates, reconsiders, grimaces, but obeys. He turns pages, runs his finger up and down, goes past the right page, goes back, at last finds the word.*)

ADAM. Okay. I've got it.

NATHAN. Read the definition. To all of us.

ADAM. This is ridiculous.

NATHAN. Read it.

ADAM. (*slowly, laboriously, intentionally without expression*) "Irony. A method of humorous or subtly sarcastic expression in which the intended meaning of the words used is the direct opposite of their usual sense. The irony of calling a stupid plan 'clever.'" There's more, but that's all I'm reading.

NATHAN. Do you understand what you just read?

ADAM. Of course I do. I'm not an idiot. But what's the point of it? Why not just call a stupid plan *stupid?*

(*There is a long silence.*)

NATHAN. Sometimes, you can make a statement even stronger by *not* saying what you mean.

MAGGIE. Make believe you understand him.

ADAM. I do. It just doesn't make sense to me.

DANIEL. Me, neither.

ADAM. I wonder if Jonathan's leaving was *his* way of not saying what he meant.

NATHAN. You're a quick study, aren't you?

DANIEL. We woke up one morning, and he was gone.

MAGGIE. Never said a word to any of us.

NATHAN. The only thing he left behind was his book.

ELEANOR. That was hard to understand.

MAGGIE. He spent all that time working on it.

DANIEL. We thought it was important to him.

NATHAN. It was.

ELEANOR. (*after a beat*) I have some leftovers from last night. Meat loaf, vegetables. I'll heat them up. We can have lunch in about ten minutes. Can I get some lemonade for you, Adam? Daniel?

ADAM. No thanks.

DANIEL. No, sweetheart.

(ELEANOR *exits.*)

DANIEL. Hey, Adam, maybe we can get that damn piece of molding off. The one in the corner. I can't move the damn thing.

(*They take some tools out of the tool kit and start working on the molding.*)

DANIEL. Adam and I got some great shots of a family of deer today.

NATHAN. That fills an important cultural need.

MAGGIE. Why don't you guys do a coffee-table book? "Deer I Have Known and Scared the Shit Out Of"?

DANIEL. You should come with us one morning, Maggie. Real early. Watch the woods wake up. Smell the fresh air. Listen to the birds.

MAGGIE. I think I'd rather spend more quality time with my hens.

DANIEL. Damn! I can't get that nail loose!

ADAM. Hold on a minute.

(*He reaches down, pulls up the leg of his jeans, unsheathes the hunting knife. He digs the knife into the wood, pulling the nail out and loosening the molding, which comes off.*)

DANIEL. (*cautiously touching the blade*) Man, that's sharp.

ADAM. What good is a knife, if it isn't sharp?

NATHAN. That's quite a weapon.

ADAM. (*Returns the knife to the ankle sheath.*) I've met some unpleasant people in my travels. No sense in being unprepared.

MAGGIE. He's full of surprises, isn't he?

ADAM. Isn't that what you like about me, Maggie?

MAGGIE. I guess it is.

ADAM. You know, Nathan, if I stick around for a while, I may surprise you—all of you—one of these days.

NATHAN. Is that so?

ADAM. I may decide to read Jonathan's book, after all. You never know.

NATHAN. Be sure to give me fair warning. Remember my weak heart.

ADAM. I may even try my hand at writing my *own* book. About a guy from Lexington, Mass, who hitch-hikes around the country.

NATHAN. That sounds vaguely familiar.

ADAM. But it would be *my* story, not Jonathan's.

NATHAN. I can hardly wait.

(*Offstage, the sound of a key turning in the lock of the front door. The door opens.* JONATHAN *enters.*)

DANIEL. Jesus Christ Almighty!

JONATHAN. No, Daniel, it's just me. I parked down the road. I wanted to surprise you.

(MAGGIE *runs to* JONATHAN, *embraces him. He doesn't respond. He pulls away, shakes* DANIEL's *hand absently, looks at* ADAM.)

JONATHAN. Who's he?

MAGGIE. Grandpa's latest project: Adam.

NATHAN. What an unpleasant surprise.

JONATHAN. It doesn't have to be.

ELEANOR. (*Enters, runs to* JONATHAN, *embraces him.*) My God, Jonathan! It's wonderful to see you again.

JONATHAN. Did you do those drawings, Maggie?

MAGGIE. Yes, I did.

JONATHAN. You're getting better.

MAGGIE. Here's the *bad* news. Someone else is sleeping on the couch now.

JONATHAN. On *my* couch?

NATHAN. On *our* couch.

ADAM. I've heard a lot about you.

JONATHAN. Nothing positive, I'll bet.

ADAM. The vanishing novelist...

JONATHAN. I want to come back. I hope I can.

NATHAN. You can't just walk in again, as if you'd never left.

ELEANOR. You look so pale. Poor dear. I'll set another place at the table.

JONATHAN. *(to ADAM)* How long have you been here?

ADAM. A few weeks.

JONATHAN. How'd they find you?

ADAM. I was hitchhiking. Daniel picked me up. Invited me to dinner.

JONATHAN. Baked ham?

ADAM. Beef stew.

JONATHAN. I like the ham better.

ADAM. It's a little too salty for my taste.

ELEANOR. Why didn't you tell me?

JONATHAN. Has Maggie hit on you yet?

ADAM. That's between her and me.

JONATHAN. So the Age of Chivalry isn't dead.

ADAM. I'm old fashioned.

JONATHAN. Did she tell you about her long-lost husband?

MAGGIE. Jonathan!

JONATHAN. (*playing* MAGGIE, *with a falsetto voice*) "He was so handsome, so perfect. Prettier than me!" (*in his normal voice*) That was mean. I'm sorry, Maggie.

DANIEL. You should be.

ADAM. Bad move, Jonathan.

NATHAN. Why did you come back?

JONATHAN. No preliminaries? No "Gee, you look great"?

MAGGIE. (*sarcastically*) Gee, you look great.

ELEANOR. How have you been?

JONATHAN. Okay. But I've been better.

ELEANOR. Poor dear.

JONATHAN. I've missed you. What you gave me. What we gave each other.

DANIEL. You never even said goodbye.

ELEANOR. We were family, Jonathan.

NATHAN. Why did you come back?

JONATHAN. I shouldn't have left.

NATHAN. And you think, just like that, we'll forgive you?

JONATHAN. I learned a lot in the past few months.

ADAM. Where've you been?

JONATHAN. In Cleveland for a while. Kansas City. Las Vegas.

ADAM. I liked Vegas. It seemed like it was always night-time there. And everything was fake, except the money.

MAGGIE. Did you stay in Vegas?

JONATHAN. Not for long. I went out to San Francisco.

NATHAN. And when you finally reached El Dorado, were the streets paved with gold?

JONATHAN. I got a job as a waiter–

NATHAN. A noble profession.

ADAM. That's what *I* did when I was out there.

JONATHAN. And when I wasn't working, I was writing.

MAGGIE. What about the girls?

JONATHAN. I didn't have the time, or the money.

ADAM. What a shame, wasting a city like that!

NATHAN. Were you working on *Family Ties*?

JONATHAN. Yes, I was.

ADAM. How ironic.

JONATHAN. After a few weeks, I realized I may have been wrong about the book.

NATHAN. Did you?

JONATHAN. I think you were right.

MAGGIE. Is that a chorus of angels I hear?

DANIEL. After all the fights–

ELEANOR. All the arguments.

JONATHAN. Then I began writing it the way *you* wanted me to.

MAGGIE. Hallelluyah!

NATHAN. And now you think we'll take you back?

JONATHAN. I hope you will.

ADAM. Do you believe him, Nathan?

NATHAN. I don't know.

JONATHAN. I understand now...

ADAM. It isn't so easy out there, is it?

JONATHAN. No, it isn't, but...

ADAM. You've got to be strong. I always knew that.

JONATHAN. This has nothing to do with you.

ADAM. I think it *does*.

NATHAN. I was trying to give you the benefit of my knowledge.

JONATHAN. I should have listened to you.

NATHAN. Maybe I was a bit harsh.

JONATHAN. There were times I couldn't write one word that you liked.

NATHAN. I can't help it. That's what teachers do.

JONATHAN. I've only finished about half the rewrite. I need your help, Grandpa.

NATHAN. I'm not sure you deserve it.

ELEANOR. He'll listen to you now, Pa.

ADAM. But does he mean it?

JONATHAN. Stay out of this!

NATHAN. I don't know if I really believe you, Jonathan.

DANIEL. I'm not sure I do, either. You hurt us, you know.

ELEANOR. We cared about you.

MAGGIE. You drove me to drink. Well, not really, but it's a hell of a good excuse.

DANIEL. How do we know you won't get tired of us again?

ADAM. How can they trust you? Here today, gone tomorrow.

JONATHAN. I told you to stay out of this.

ADAM. Just trying to help.

JONATHAN. You don't know if you can trust me?

NATHAN. You left us once.

DANIEL. You could do it again.

ADAM. And that would be even worse.

JONATHAN. What about *you*, Grandpa? Should I trust *you*?

NATHAN. Why not?

JONATHAN. When I first got to San Francisco, I was still angry at you. Very angry. Then, day after day, little by little, the anger died. I realized I was wrong. So I started on the road back. But I had to make one stop.

ADAM. Where?

JONATHAN. Stratfield College.

NATHAN. Stratfield?

JONATHAN. I wanted to see the place where you'd spent so many years of your life. I wanted to feel a part of it. A part of *you*. I thought I could get to know you better that way.

ADAM. Not a bad idea.

(*As* JONATHAN *speaks, he acts out his visit to the campus.*)

JONATHAN. I walked around the campus for a while, up onto that grassy hill behind the auditorium. I could see all the way to the lake. Then I went over to the reflecting pool under that huge oak tree. I sat there for a while, Grandpa, imagining one of those outdoor classes you told me about. I could picture you there, with your students on the grass all around you, soaking up every word. Then I went through the old stone arch to the library, and it was just like you said it was. My last stop was the English Department office. I told them I wanted to contact an old professor of mine. I gave them your name. Guess what?

ADAM. I can hardly wait.

JONATHAN. (*in an official voice, playing the part of the clerk in the English Department office*) "I'm sorry. There never was a professor by that name at Stratfield. Never."

DANIEL. Goddamn!

ADAM. (*softly, to himself*) Goddamn.

ELEANOR. You shouldn't have done that, Jonathan.

JONATHAN. (*in the same official voice*) "There was an Assistant Registrar by that name, who worked at the college. Not a teacher, just one of our paper pushers."

MAGGIE. It doesn't matter.

JONATHAN. (*in the same official voice*) "He got sick, five or six years ago. I'm not sure what it was. Something wrong with his heart. So he retired... We gave him a nice gold watch. He took his pension, and left for who knows where."

ADAM. *We* know where.

JONATHAN. (*in his own voice*) Not a teacher. Not a guide to generations of budding scholars and authors. Just a "liar." We don't have to look up that word in your big dictionary, do we, Grandpa?

NATHAN. I could have taught their classes better than any of them. I knew more than any of them.

ELEANOR. Of course you did.

NATHAN. (*his voice gradually growing in volume, as his anger grows*) When I went to college, the business courses were easy for me—management, marketing. My father told me to stick with those "easy" courses. He was a professor—the chairman of the English Department, and he had been a Rhodes Scholar. Everyone told me how brilliant he was. And he never stopped telling me how disappointed he was in me.

DANIEL. A father shouldn't do that.

NATHAN. I wasn't as smart as he was, but he didn't have to keep telling me that! And in class, when it mattered, when it really mattered, when it was literature, or philosophy, I always froze up. On exams, too. The professor's voice was always my father's voice, arrogant, mocking me. I could never organize my thoughts. I always ran out of time.

ELEANOR. It doesn't matter now, Pa.

NATHAN. I couldn't think, damn it! But I'm not stupid. I'm not!

ELEANOR. Of course, you're not.

NATHAN. Later, when I was working at Stratfield, I began to study on my own, to learn on my own, and I've kept learning. I've never stopped learning.

JONATHAN. Why did you have to lie to me?

NATHAN. Is the truth so important?

ADAM. Good question.

ELEANOR. He *could* have been a teacher.

MAGGIE. A *marvelous* teacher.

DANIEL. A *great* teacher.

ADAM. But he *wasn't*. Does that matter to you, Jonathan?

JONATHAN. Leave us alone. This has nothing to do with you.

ADAM. That's not true. *I'm* sleeping on the couch now.

JONATHAN. Maybe you'd better start packing your bags.

ADAM. I'd rather not.

MAGGIE. A couple of weeks ago, we didn't have *any*. Now we've got one too many.

JONATHAN. I want to come back, Grandpa.

NATHAN. Do you?

JONATHAN. I need this family. *My* family. We need each other. Isn't that so?

DANIEL. For how long will you need us? I wonder.

JONATHAN. I want your help, Grandpa.

NATHAN. You want my help...

JONATHAN. But without the lies. We've cleared the air.

ELEANOR. I think it'd be all right, Pa. I do.

NATHAN. Maybe... Maybe it would be.

MAGGIE. Or maybe he'll pull another disappearing act.

DANIEL. What if you get mad at Grandpa again? What if you get tired of us again?

JONATHAN. I won't, Daniel. I won't.

ELEANOR. It could be better than before.

JONATHAN. Yes, Eleanor, it could be.

ADAM. Before everyone kisses and makes up, I've got a question.

JONATHAN. I told you to back off.

ADAM. Don't talk that way, Jonathan. I'm beginning to take it personally.

JONATHAN. You think I give a damn how you take it?

MAGGIE. Jonathan, relax. You're not the macho type.

ADAM. So here we are, Jonathan and I, in a quiet little house in the woods—the house of a make-believe professor. But why bother to fool us? Who cares whether Nathan really was a teacher or not?

ELEANOR. *He* cares.

ADAM. And the rest of you don't mind making believe with him?

JONATHAN. Leave him alone. It's not that big a lie.

ADAM. Where did that sudden flash of generosity come from?

ELEANOR. Leave us alone, Adam.

ADAM. You know that Nathan was never a teacher. Why all that respect for him, that admiration? That love?

DANIEL. That's what makes us a family. That's what keeps us together.

ADAM. But don't you have to *earn* respect and love?

DANIEL. No, we don't have to earn it. It's just part of who we are.

ELEANOR. We love each other. We love Grandpa.

ADAM. For being a liar? Is that how he got to be God?

DANIEL. It's not up to you—

ELEANOR. —To judge us.

DANIEL. You don't understand us, Adam.

ADAM. Don't you care about the truth?

NATHAN. (*angrily*) Do you think I'm the only liar here?

ELEANOR. Pa, let it be.

DANIEL. Please, Nathan...

NATHAN. It's all right for *me* to be humiliated...

MAGGIE. Grandpa...

ADAM. Who else is lying, Nathan?

NATHAN. They're *all* lying.

ELEANOR. Pa—

NATHAN. "Pa"? That's lie number one.

ADAM. You're not Eleanor's father?

ELEANOR. Don't!

DANIEL. No more, Nathan!

MAGGIE. No more!

ADAM. Is it a lie, Nathan?

NATHAN. It's a lie.

JONATHAN. What the hell is he talking about?

ADAM. Speak up, Nathan. Now we *both* want to know.

DANIEL. There's nothing to know.

NATHAN. We're all liars.

ADAM. There seems to be a difference of opinion here. I'll put my money on the old man.

ELEANOR. We don't care what you believe.

JONATHAN. Is Nathan your father?

DANIEL. Let it be, Jonathan.

ELEANOR. I want you to come back. I want you to write those beautiful poems for me again.

ADAM. Is he your father?

ELEANOR. (*remembering* JONATHAN's *poem*) "The first of May, we went out Maying, she and I,/ As if she needed an excuse for me to love her./ And she was all young and—"

JONATHAN. Tell me the truth!

DANIEL. Why the hell does it matter? Everyone lies! About how old they are. Or how much they weigh. Or how well they did in school.

ADAM. Or who their father is?

DANIEL. (*softly*) Even that.

ELEANOR. We needed a family. So did he.

ADAM. Are you and Daniel married?

DANIEL. Of course we are.

MAGGIE. You don't have to tell them anything.

DANIEL. Don't be afraid, Maggie.

ADAM. When did you meet Nathan?

DANIEL. About four years ago.

MAGGIE. Daddy...

DANIEL. It's all right.

NATHAN. When I retired, the pension money didn't amount to much. I went to live with my brother in Hartford. He lived in a rundown neighborhood. Drug dealers. Prostitutes. Barbarians.

ADAM. Sounds charming.

NATHAN. He was older—and sicker—than me. I was one old man taking care of another, in a neighborhood where I was afraid to go out at night.

ADAM. The golden years.

JONATHAN. And what did you teach your brother? How to die in bed?

ADAM. Low blow.

MAGGIE. Grandpa...

NATHAN. Liars, all liars.

MAGGIE. Just a little make-believe.

ADAM. Go on, Nathan. Tell us.

NATHAN. Should I answer him, Eleanor? Or do you want to? We share everything in our family, don't we?

JONATHAN. (*mocking the* words) Our "family"...

NATHAN. (*bitterly*) You really must forgive them. They're a little sensitive about their *own* failings.

ADAM. Tell us all about it, Nathan.

NATHAN. When I lived there—in Hartford—I used to go out every morning and buy the paper, and get a cup of coffee at this newsstand...this little store. A minor pleasure.

DANIEL. I still remember how much we looked forward to seeing you every day.

ELEANOR. You always had something interesting to tell us.

DANIEL. You knew so much about so many things.

ADAM. Fun in Hartford.

DANIEL. I had worked in a supermarket for a lot of years. Just a few blocks from our apartment. It wasn't a great job, but it was a job.

ELEANOR. When the neighborhood started to go bad, they closed the place. He lost his job.

DANIEL. I complained to the union, but they couldn't do anything about it. They said I might be able to find a spot at another market in another town.

ELEANOR. But they didn't know *when*.

DANIEL. I was so tired of the grind, of taking crap all the time.

ADAM. Aren't we all?

ELEANOR. We sold the only valuable thing we owned: the piano that my mother had left me.

DANIEL. I cashed out my union pension. And we were able to borrow some money to buy the store. We used the store as collateral.

ELEANOR. We thought it would pay off, in the long run. And we'd be our own bosses, anyway.

ADAM. The great American dream.

DANIEL. The money was okay. But the work was exhausting.

ELEANOR. For both of us, every day – long hours. I hated it.

DANIEL. But as I said, the money was pretty good. And then, after a few months, we met "Fancy Dan." We had the same name. It was as if he was another version of *me*.

JONATHAN. Fancy Dan? It sounds like some kind of joke.

ELEANOR. That's what he called himself. And he was no joke.

DANIEL. (*As DANIEL describes Fancy Dan, he becomes Fancy Dan, standing taller, moving sinuously.*) A tall man. Slim. Moved like a snake. Always well dressed. Shoes shined. Manicured. Dark glasses, so you could never see his eyes.

ELEANOR. He spoke very softly, almost in a whisper.

NATHAN. When he smiled at you, it made you shiver.

DANIEL. He came in one afternoon. Picked up a newspaper. (*in Fancy Dan's soft voice*) "Black coffee, please. Real sweet."

ELEANOR. But he didn't pay for anything.

DANIEL. He looked at me and smiled. (*As Fancy Dan, he approaches* ADAM, *as if* ADAM *is now playing* DANIEL.) He said, "They call me

'Fancy Dan.' But you can call me 'Fancy.' You got that? *Remember* that."

ELEANOR. Then he walked out.

DANIEL. "Remember that."

ELEANOR. There were always two or three other men waiting for him outside. They never came into the store. They just watched and waited.

ADAM. He kept coming back?

DANIEL. Every day. Usually late in the afternoon, when it was quiet.

NATHAN. I used to see him there sometimes.

ELEANOR. He started to take cigarettes, candy, magazines.

DANIEL. One day he said, "I've got some people to meet. Some business to do. I'm going to do it here."

JONATHAN. Was he selling drugs?

DANIEL. Yes. And guns, too.

JONATHAN. You should have told the cops.

ADAM. That's a *terrific* idea, Jonathan. You must have been the pride of your Boy Scout troop.

MAGGIE. Is there a Merit Badge for stupidity?

DANIEL. Then, one day, Eleanor said something Fancy didn't like.

ELEANOR. I was tired. I was afraid. I just asked him to leave us alone— *asked* him, not told him.

DANIEL. He said, "I do what I fancy. I always do what I fancy." And he put his hands on her, around her throat.

(DANIEL *puts his hands around* ADAM's *throat.*)

ELEANOR. His fingers were barely touching me. But I thought I was going to die.

DANIEL. I shouted his name. "Fancy, you want to kill someone, kill me!"

ELEANOR. He let go of me. (DANIEL *releases* ADAM.) He spun around to face Daniel.

DANIEL. (*acting out the violence*) I hit him across the bridge of the nose and again on the side of his face. His sunglasses flew off. I could see his eyes for the first time—the anger in them—the hatred.

ELEANOR. Daniel kept hitting him, over and over again.

DANIEL. He lay still for a minute. I stood over him. My knuckles were raw and bloody—his blood and mine.

ELEANOR. Then, suddenly, he was on his feet again—

DANIEL. With a knife in his hand.

ELEANOR. The blade was long and thin. It was shining so brightly...

DANIEL. (*As Fancy Dan again,* DANIEL *pantomimes the attack, using* ADAM *as his victim.*) He cut my hand, my cheek. And he backed me up against the wall with the knife at my throat. He said, very softly, (*in Fancy's voice*) "Fancy could kill you now. Or tomorrow. Or the next day."

ELEANOR. Then he left. (*reliving the fear*) The *blood* on Daniel's face...

ADAM. Why didn't he kill you?

DANIEL. I think he wanted to take the time to enjoy it.

ELEANOR. We couldn't stay there any longer.

DANIEL. I closed the place.

ELEANOR. A big company that had a chain of newsstands in Hartford was after us to sell. We did.

ADAM. Why did he let you get away?

DANIEL. Somebody got to him first. Word on the street was that one of his own men took a "fancy" to being the boss.

ELEANOR. He just disappeared.

DANIEL. And so did *we*.

NATHAN. Daniel had talked to me about leaving the city, living out in the woods, where you could breathe clean air.

DANIEL. And see the sky.

JONATHAN. So "Grandpa" is just a joke.

NATHAN. I was never married. Never had a child.

ADAM. What about Maggie?

ELEANOR. It would have been easier for me if there had been a child for me to love.

MAGGIE. You don't have to tell them every fucking thing!

DANIEL. It turned out we couldn't have children.

ELEANOR. (*sadly*) You really didn't want kids anyway, did you?

DANIEL. I thought it would be one more burden for me. But finally—finally I understood how much it meant to you. I'm sorry it took me so long.

ADAM. So Maggie was an afterthought.

JONATHAN. Another joke.

MAGGIE. (*softly*) My father died when I was six. By the time I was sixteen, my mother was on her third husband. She may be on her fourth—or is it her fifth by now. That's just hearsay. We don't keep in touch. *This* is my family.

NATHAN. Liars, all liars.

ADAM. Where did you find Maggie?

DANIEL. She lived in an apartment in our building.

ELEANOR. She worked the night shift at a diner.

MAGGIE. The *Dead-End* Diner.

DANIEL. She used to come into our place in the afternoon.

ELEANOR. We got to know her. I felt that she needed me. I needed *her*, too.

MAGGIE. We started to talk about things—the things that mattered to us.

ELEANOR. Like how lonely we were.

MAGGIE. Please, Momma...

ELEANOR. We both needed a family. I needed a child to love. We found Maggie.

MAGGIE. Every family does the same thing. They hand out the parts, like in a movie or a play. "You be the good kid, and she'll be the bad one." "You be the wise old grandfather. She'll be the nice, loving mother." We're no different.

JONATHAN. The perfect family.

ADAM. Whose idea was it to come here? Yours, Nathan?

DANIEL. We sort of hatched it together.

NATHAN. My brother died, finally. He left me a lot more money than I thought he had. We could have lived much better.

DANIEL. I hated the city, the look of it, the smell of it.

ELEANOR. We had to get away.

NATHAN. I told Daniel about the money I'd inherited.

DANIEL. And I already had a buyer for the store.

ADAM. Did you want to come here, too, Maggie?

MAGGIE. Not at first.

ELEANOR. But by then, we were closer. Much closer.

MAGGIE. She said she didn't want to leave me behind.

ELEANOR. Of course not. I couldn't leave my—daughter—behind.

DANIEL. We're family.

ELEANOR. Daniel told me she could come with us.

NATHAN. He said we could all be together. That we could be what we *wanted* to be. To *ourselves*. To each *other*.

MAGGIE. That we could *stay* together.

ADAM. And Nathan would call the shots?

DANIEL. That's what he's supposed to do. That's who he's supposed to *be*. He's a lot smarter than I am. He *should* call the shots.

JONATHAN. *(snidely)* After all, he was a college professor.

ELEANOR. He could teach me about music and other things I always wanted to know about.

MAGGIE. And no matter what I did or said, I would never have to leave. I would always have my family.

DANIEL. Always. That's the way I—the way *we* wanted it.

MAGGIE. We take care of each other.

ADAM. You don't seem very happy.

MAGGIE. It's better than being alone.

DANIEL. Much better.

JONATHAN. So that's the game.

MAGGIE. All we need is each other.

ADAM. You need more than that, don't you? You need Jonathan. Or me. A son, I suppose. A grandson. A lover.

JONATHAN. A disciple.

ADAM. Someone to believe the lies.

JONATHAN. You all wanted a piece of me. You didn't care about what *I* wanted. You were so busy inventing yourselves.

DANIEL. Most people live in a make-believe world, Jonathan.

JONATHAN. *I* can't. I *won't*.

ADAM. Sounds like Jonathan's disappointed in you.

JONATHAN. I shouldn't have come back.

NATHAN. But you *can* come back now, Jonathan.

DANIEL. I don't think I want him back, Nathan. I don't trust him.

MAGGIE. I don't want him back either.

NATHAN. We could work together.

JONATHAN. When I was out in San Francisco—and even after I knew about Grandpa's lie—it didn't really matter that much. I needed him. I wanted to come home.

ELEANOR. You can do that now, dear.

JONATHAN. I wanted to come back to my family.

ELEANOR. We can be—we *are* your family.

DANIEL. Eleanor...

JONATHAN. I don't know *who* the hell you are.

ADAM. They *want* to be a family.

JONATHAN. That's not enough. Too many lies.

MAGGIE. We don't need you.

JONATHAN. Hey, I've got a whole new take on *Family Ties*. A whole new angle.

NATHAN. I can help you with it.

JONATHAN. You already have.

MAGGIE. I wish we hadn't.

JONATHAN. I'm going to write about *this* family. You're not real people. You're make-believe. You *belong* in a novel.

DANIEL. That's not fair, Jonathan.

JONATHAN. It's a great story. A bunch of losers get together to make believe they're a family. To invent a world where they feel important. Where they feel safe. Where they feed off each other.

DANIEL. You shouldn't do that.

NATHAN. Jonathan, don't go.

JONATHAN. Nothing here is real.

DANIEL. Let him go, Nathan.

ELEANOR. We don't *have* to make believe, do we, Daniel?

DANIEL. Yes, we do, Eleanor.

NATHAN. You can stay, Jonathan.

ADAM. And I was just getting comfortable on the couch.

JONATHAN. You're welcome to it.

NATHAN. You don't have to go.

JONATHAN. I can't wait to start my *new* book.

NATHAN. Running away again? *That* hasn't changed, has it?

JONATHAN. I'm not running...

ELEANOR. You don't have to leave.

(JONATHAN *walks toward the front door.*)

DANIEL. Let him go. (JONATHAN *exits.*) Adam, do you want to stay here with us?

ADAM. I think so. Yes. Your lies don't really bother me. I've told a few myself.

DANIEL. Do you want to be part of our family? There's a place for you here.

MAGGIE. What are you doing, Daddy?

ADAM. A place for me? I guess I may be getting tired of being alone out there.

ELEANOR. (*frightened*) Daniel?

DANIEL. If you want to stay, you have to do something for us.

ADAM. You don't want Jonathan to go.

DANIEL. I don't want him to write that *book*. It wouldn't be fair to us. Our lies haven't hurt anyone.

ADAM. (*Pulls his knife from the ankle sheath, runs toward front door.*) Until now.

(ADAM *exits.*)

ELEANOR. What are you doing, Dan?

DANIEL. I'm protecting our family.

MAGGIE. You shouldn't have told them, Grandpa.

NATHAN. (*wearily*) I'm sorry. So sorry.

DANIEL. It's all right. We're still a family.

NATHAN. (*muttering*) Still a family.

ELEANOR. I'm afraid again, Daniel.

DANIEL. Don't be.

ELEANOR. But you're inviting Fancy to live with us.

NATHAN. The barbarians...

DANIEL. (*confidently*) Don't worry about Adam. I can handle him.

MAGGIE. We still love each other.

DANIEL. And we always will.

(*Long beat. Sound of front door opening and closing.* ADAM *enters. He's holding the knife in his hand. He walks to the dining room table, picks up a napkin, wipes the blade of the knife, returns it to its sheath.*)

NATHAN. (*moaning*) Jonathan...

DANIEL. We've got some things to do, Adam.

ADAM. Right. We'll find a nice, quiet spot in the woods for Jonathan.

ELEANOR. God...

DANIEL. What about his car?

ADAM. I'll take care of that.

MAGGIE. What's happening, Daddy?

DANIEL. We're surviving.

ELEANOR. Is that enough?

DANIEL. Yes, sweetheart, it's enough.

ADAM. We've got to stick together. Help each other. That's what families are for. Isn't that right, Daniel? Isn't that right, Grandpa?

MAGGIE. For God's sake, Adam.

ADAM. For our *family's* sake.

DANIEL. For our family's sake.

ADAM. I'll be Grandpa's student. And Maggie's lover. I'll teach you how to play Chopin, Eleanor. I'll wander in the woods with you, Daniel, if that's what you want. I'll help with the chores, too. I've worked on a farm before. I won't even insist on sleeping in one of the bedrooms. The couch'll do fine. For now.

DANIEL. The couch'll do fine for as long as you stay here.

ADAM. Will it?

DANIEL. (*taking command*) This is *my* house, Adam. *My* family. *My* rules.

ADAM. And what if I want to change the rules?

DANIEL. I guess you'll have to ask Jonathan about that. Or maybe it would be better to ask Fancy.

MAGGIE. Fancy?

DANIEL. Fancy taught me how to survive.

MAGGIE. Daddy?

DANIEL. The word on the street about what happened to him—was wrong.

MAGGIE. I don't believe you.

ADAM. (*after a beat*) I do.

DANIEL. Eleanor, how about that lunch? You'll probably have to re-heat it. (DANIEL *walks to the cabinet, takes out two bottles of wine.*) What's your pleasure, Grandpa? A Merlot? A Cabernet?

ADAM. Why don't *you* pick it, Daniel? This is *your* party, isn't it?

END